STL for C++
Programmers

STL for C++ Programmers

Leen Ammeraal
Hogeschool Utrecht, The Netherlands

JOHN WILEY & SONS
Chichester • New York • Weinheim • Brisbane • Toronto • Singapore

Other Wiley Editorial Offices

John Wiley & Sons, Inc., 605 Third Avenue,
New York, NY 10158-0012, USA

Wiley-VCH Verlag GmbH, Pappelallee 3,
D-69469 Weinheim, Germany

Jacaranda Wiley Ltd, 33 Park Road, Milton,
Queensland 4064, Australia

John Wiley & Sons (Canada) Ltd, 22 Worcester Road,
Rexdale, Ontario M9W 1L1, Canada

John Wiley & Sons (Asia) Pte Ltd, 2 Clementi Loop #02-01
Jin Xing Distripark, Singapore 129 809

British Library Cataloguing in Publication Data
A catalogue record for this book is available from the British Library

ISBN   0 471 97181 2

Produced from PostScript files supplied by the author.
Printed and bound in Great Britain by Bookcraft (Bath) Ltd, Midsomer Norton, Somerset.
This book is printed on acid-free paper responsibly manufactured from sustainable forestry, in which at least two trees are planted for each one used for paper production.

Contents

Preface

When templates were introduced in the C++ language some years ago, few C++ programmers were aware of the influence this concept would have on the standard library. The Standard Template Library was originally designed by A. A. Stepanov and M. Lee both of Hewlett-Packard, and D. R. Musser, of Rensselaer Polytechnic Institute. After having made some minor modifications, the C++ Standards Committee adopted STL, making it a substantial part of the standard library.

The use of STL is likely to make software more reliable, more portable and more general and to reduce the cost of producing it. No professional C++ programmer can therefore afford to ignore this library. I wrote this book for those programmers and for others who are already reasonably familiar with C++.

This book is about the standard version of STL, not the original HP version. You can download the example programs, not only to save typing work but also to avoid portability problems: some of the downloadable program versions have been made more portable by using conditional compilation to work around non-standard behavior of current STL versions from Microsoft and Borland. The examples are available as a singe file, *stlcpp.zip*, from my web site

   http://www.econ.hvu.nl/~ammeraal/

or directly from either of these ftp sites:

   ftp://ftp.expa.fnt.hvu.nl/pub/ammeraal/
   ftp://pitel-lnx.ibk.fnt.hvu.nl/pub/ammeraal/

I am grateful to Gaynor Redvers-Mutton of Wiley and Francis Glassborow of the Association of C & C++ Users, who encouraged me to write this book and who made some useful suggestions about its contents.

Leen Ammeraal

1

STL for Beginners

1.1 Templates, Namespaces and Type *bool*

As its name suggests, the Standard Template Library (STL) is based on the comparatively new subject of *templates*. We will therefore begin with a brief discussion of this subject.

Template functions

Suppose that for some positive number x we frequently want to compute the expression

```
2 * x + (x * x + 1) / (2 * x)
```

where x can be either *double* or *int*. In the latter case the division operator / denotes integer division, giving an integer result. For example, if x has type *double* and is equal to 5.0, the value of the above expression is 12.6, but if x has type *int* and is equal to 5, that value is 12. Instead of writing two functions, such as

```
double f(double x)
{   double x2 = 2 * x;
    return x2 + (x * x + 1)/x2;
}

int f(int x)
{   int x2 = 2 * x;
    return x2 + (x * x + 1)/x2;
}
```

we can write only one *template*, as the following complete program shows:

```
// ftempl.cpp: A template function.
#include <iostream.h>

template <class T>
T f(T x)
{   T x2 = 2 * x;
    return x2 + (x * x + 1)/x2;
}

int main()
{   cout << f(5.0) << endl << f(5) << endl;
    return 0;
}
```

The output of this program is

```
12.6
12
```

In the template, T denotes a type, given by the argument in the call of f. Here the call $f(5.0)$ causes *double* (the type of 5.0) to be taken for T, so that, for example, floating-point division is used in $(x * x + 1)/x2$. By contrast, T stands for *int* when the call $f(5)$ is performed, resulting in integer division.

When dealing with program *ftempl.cpp*, the compiler generates two separate functions, much similar to the functions $f(double)$ and $f(int)$ we started with. It follows that the compiler must 'see' both the template definition and the template calls at the same time. This makes templates bad candidates for being compiled separately; instead, we normally place templates in header files. If we use such header files written by others, we see very little of the templates themselves, and we call them just like normal functions, as the calls $f(5.0)$ and $f(5)$ in our program illustrate. When using STL function templates, we are therefore hardly aware that we are calling functions generated from templates.

What's in a name?

A template such as the one above, starting with the word *template* and ending at the closing brace that follows the return-statement, was originally called a *function template* by Stroustrup, the designer of C++. This term expresses that we are dealing with a certain kind of template, to be distinguished from class templates, to be discussed in a moment. These days many authors use the word *template function* instead, because these templates are much like conventional functions. We will also adopt this term *template function* in this book, and we will sometimes even use the shorter term *function* for them. The same applies to the notion discussed below, originally called a *class template*, but referred to as a *template class* or even simply as a *class* in this book.

Templates classes

We can use type parameters (such as *T*) for classes in about the same way as we did for functions. Suppose we want a class *Pair*, to store pairs of numbers. Sometimes both numbers are of type *double*, sometimes they are of type *int*. Then instead of two new classes, say,

```
class PairDouble {
public:
    PairDouble(double x1, double y1): x(x1), y(y1){}
    void showQ();
private:
    double x, y;
};

void PairDouble::showQ()
{  cout << x/y << endl;
}
```

followed by a similar fragment for class *PairInt*, we can write only one *template class*, as the following complete program demonstrates:

```
// cltempl.cpp: A template class.
#include <iostream.h>

template <class T>
class Pair {
public:
    Pair(T x1, T y1): x(x1), y(y1){}
    void showQ();
private:
    T x, y;
};

template <class T>
void Pair<T>::showQ()
{  cout << x/y << endl;
}

int main()
{  Pair<double> a(37.0, 5.0);
    Pair<int> u(37, 5);
    a.showQ();
    u.showQ();
    return 0;
}
```

The way template class member functions, such as *showQ*, are defined outside the class may at first look very complicated. But this notation is really very logical: the name of any member function defined outside its class must be immediately preceded by the part

type ::

and it is reasonable that in this case we should write *Pair<T>* for *type*. Besides, as STL users we need not always bother about such definitions, since the STL template classes are available as header files that we can use without understanding every programming detail. The only typical template aspect we see in our programs is the actual type we provide in notations such as *Pair<double>*.

Namespaces

There is another new language element, *namespaces*, which we cannot ignore. If a program consists of many files, we must be careful to avoid *name clashes*. The namespace concept can be very helpful in this regard. In the following program, there are two global variables *i*, which do not clash because they are in distinct namespaces:

```
// namespac.cpp: The namespace concept.
#include <iostream.h>

namespace A
{ int i = 10;
}

namespace B
{ int i = 20;
}

void fA()
{   using namespace A;
    cout << "In fA:    " <<
      A::i << " " << B::i << " " << i << endl;
}

void fB()
{   using namespace B;
    cout << "In fB:    " <<
      A::i << " " << B::i << " " << i << endl;
}

int main()
{   fA(); fB();
    cout << "In main: " << A::i << " " << B::i << endl;
    // cout << i << endl; This would be invalid here.
    using A::i;
    cout << i << endl; // But this is valid.
    return 0;
}
```

This program produces the following output:

```
In fA:    10 20 10
In fB:    10 20 20
In main: 10 20
10
```

Thanks to the identifiers *A* and *B*, we can later refer to these namespaces. For namespace *A*, we can write either something of the form

```
A:: ...
```

or one of the statements

```
using namespace A;
using A::i;
```

Only after one of the latter two statements does the unqualified identifier *i* refer to the variable *i* (with value 10) defined in the namespace *A*. The output of this program demonstrates this.

Type *bool*: synonymous with *int* or a built-in type?

Type *bool* and its two possible values *true* and *false* are defined in the original STL header files in the following, conventional way, also found in many C programs:

```
#define bool int
#define true 1
#define false 0
```

However, according to the Draft C++ Standard, *bool* is really a built-in type, which implies that the following program, not using any header file, should compile:

```
int main()
{  bool b;
   return 0;
}
```

Some older compilers will not accept this program because they do not recognize *bool* as a built-in type.

According to the Draft C++ Standard, the types *bool* and *int* are *not* identical, as the following typical output of program *boolint.cpp* illustrates:

```
sizeof(bool) = 1
sizeof(int) = 4
With B defined as bool B[100], we have
sizeof(B) = 100
```

The program that produces this output is shown below:

```
// boolint.cpp: Types bool and int are not identical.
#include <iostream.h>

int main()
{   cout << "sizeof(bool) = " << sizeof(bool) << endl;
    cout << "sizeof(int) = " << sizeof(int) << endl;
    bool B[100];
    cout << "With B defined as bool B[100], we have\n";
    cout << "sizeof(B) = " << sizeof(B) << endl;
    return 0;
}
```

Apparently, each *bool* array element takes a byte, while, with 32-bit words, it would take four bytes if the types *bool* and *int* were synonymous. You might have expected an even more economical representation, with eight *bool* array elements stored in a single byte, but that would slow down the operations on these elements.

We will discuss some more differences between C++ (and STL) versions in the next section.

1.2 Starting with STL

After installing a modern C++ compiler, we can immediately use STL, so that, for example, we can compile and run the following demonstration program. This reads a variable number of nonzero integers from the keyboard, and displays these, in the same order, as soon as 0 is entered. This may seem to be a very trivial task, but it is not because no limit is imposed on the number of integers that are entered:

```
// readwr.cpp: Reading and writing a variable number of
//    nonzero integers (followed in the input by 0).
#include <iostream>
#include <vector>
using namespace std;

int main()
{   vector<int> v;
    int x;
    cout << "Enter positive integers, followed by 0:\n";
    while (cin >> x, x != 0)
      v.push_back(x);
    vector<int>::iterator i;
    for (i=v.begin(); i != v.end(); ++i)
      cout << *i << " ";
    cout << endl;
    return 0;
}
```

We can regard the *vector* template as an array of variable length. Initially this length is zero. Since we want the vector elements to be of type *int*, we consistently write *vector<int>* to denote the class we are dealing with. The statement

```
v.push_back(x);
```

adds the *int* value *x* at the end of the vector *v*.

The for-statement in this program is similar to the one in the following fragment, which displays array *a* instead of vector *v*:

```
int a[N], *p;
...
for (p=a; p != a+N; p++)
   cout << *p << " ";
```

Recall that the expressions &*a*[0] and *a* are equivalent and so are the expressions &*a*[*N*] and *a* + *N*. Starting with the first element, we traverse the array until we are past the end: although we are referring to the address of *a*[*N*], the final element is *a*[*N*–1]. This may look a dangerous thing to do, but since we are not really using the value of *a*[*N*] but only its address, this practice is perfectly safe. The variable *i*, defined as

```
vector<int>::iterator i;
```

is called an *iterator*. It works much in the same way as pointer *p* in the above fragment. The iterator value for the first element of vector *v* is denoted by the expression *v.begin*( ), the one for the element just after the final one by *v.end*( ). The vector element referred to by a well-defined iterator *i* is denoted **i*, as if *i* were a pointer. Also, the operators ++ and –– are defined for the above iterator *i*, both as post- and pre-increment versions. This explains the following for-loop:

```
for (i=v.begin(); i != v.end(); ++i)
   cout << *i << " ";
```

We had better *not* replace != with < in this loop; although this works correctly in this case, the operator < would not be correct for some types other than *vector<int>*, as we will see in Section 1.9, while the operator != works in all cases.

It is usual in mathematics to write [*a*, *b*] for the closed interval $a \le x \le b$, while we write (*a*, *b*) for the open interval $a < x < b$. This explains the notation

[*a*, *b*)

for the interval

$a \le x < b$

Likewise, we will sometimes write

   [*ia*, *ib*)

for the range of iterator values used for *i* in this fragment:

```
vector<int>::iterator i, ia, ib;
...
for (i = ia; i != ib; ++i) ...
```

Memory-allocation failure

Since all integers read by program *readwr.cpp* are stored in dynamically allocated memory, the computer system that we are using will impose a limit on the amount of input. A complicating factor with some operating systems is the use of virtual memory, which implies the use of a hard disk as an extension of RAM. Although this principle seems to provide an enormous amount of memory (at the cost of computing speed), it will be clear that sooner or later the fragment

```
vector<int> v;
for (;;) v.push_back(0);
```

will cause memory-allocation failure. This is similar to executing

```
int *p;
for(;;) p = new int;
```

In the latter fragment, the traditional test *if* (p != *NULL*), will not work with modern C++ compilers. According to the Draft C++ Standard, memory-allocation failure will not result in a pointer value *NULL* but rather 'throw an exception'. Although memory-allocation failure is a C++ (not an STL) subject, it would be important enough to discuss it here if there was a simple, portable solution, supported by most popular compilers and in accordance with a definitive C++ standard. With different compilers requiring different solutions and only a *draft* C++ standard being available, we will ignore this subject in this book, which, after all, is about STL, not about C++.

Going backward

The recommended use of != (or ==) rather than <, <=, >, >= for comparisons of iterator values makes it rather tricky to traverse the vector elements in the reverse order, using only the means we have been discussing. In program *readwr.cpp*, we could do this by replacing the for-statement with the following fragment:

```
i = v.end();
if (i != v.begin())
   do cout << *--i << " "; while (i != v.begin());
```

In this solution, the extra test at the beginning is required in case of an empty vector, that is, when 0 is the only integer entered by the user of the program. Fortunately, there is a simpler way to traverse a vector (and other data structures) from back to front. It requires the use of two other member functions, *rbegin* and *rend*, as well as a different iterator type, *reverse_iterator*, as this fragment demonstrates:

```
vector<int>::reverse_iterator i;
for (i=v.rbegin(); i != v.rend(); ++i)
    cout << *i << " ";
```

Note that we write *++i* here, not *−−i*.

New language elements and portability problems

In program *readwr.cpp*, the way header files are specified in *#include* lines may be different from what you are used to (and from the way we wrote header-file names in Section 1.1). Traditionally, we had to write *iostream.h* and *vector.h* instead of just *iostream* and *vector*. These shorter forms are new in the latest version of C++, referred to as the *Draft C++ Standard*. In many cases, we can use either notation, writing, for example, either *<iostream.h>* or *<iostream>*. From now on, we will normally use the latter, newer form.

Curiously enough, although we write *<iostream>*, the actual file name may be *iostream.h* (as is the case with Borland C++ 5.2). It is therefore doubtful whether we can call *iostream* a header *file*. From now on, we will therefore use the term *header*, rather than *header file*. Conforming to general usage, we will apply this shorter term not only to names between angular brackets, as in *<iostream>*, but also to the actual files, such as *iostream.h*.

Another new language aspect is the *using namespace std* statement near the beginning of the program. If we omit it, an error message such as *Undefined symbol 'vector'* may appear. The advantage of this namespace concept, discussed in Section 1.1, is that identifiers such as *vector* do not 'pollute the global namespace'; in other words, we may use words such as *vector* at the global level for any other purpose. If we do, we can resolve the resulting ambiguity by writing *::vector* for the global version and *std::vector* for the STL version.

Two popular C++ compilers

Both Visual C++ 5.0 (VC5) and Borland C++ 5.2 (BC5) support namespaces. STL is fully integrated in their libraries, so that no special action is required to enable its use. Most people will use this compiler from the integrated development environment, in which we can edit the program files, compile them, and so on. Instead, we can compile and link at the command-line prompt by using the commands *cl* or *bcc*32.

To make this possible, the directory path, such as

```
c:\progra~1\devstudio\vc\bin
```

or

```
c:\progra~1\borland\cbuilder\bin
```

must occur in the *path* command line in our *autoexec.bat* file. With VC5 it is also necessary to enter the command

```
vcvars32
```

to tell the compiler where to look for include files and libraries.

STL versions

The original version of STL from Hewlett-Packard Company is the basis of a considerable part of the Draft C++ Standard. This original version can be downloaded from the Internet and freely used and modified under the very weak conditions pointed out in the following copyright notice:

The version of STL incorporated in the Draft C++ Standard differs from the original one (which we will refer to as the HP STL) in the number and names of the headers. Instead of 48 files in HP STL, there are only 13 in the Draft C++ Standard, as the following table shows.

Original HP STL headers			*Standard STL*
algo.h	algobase.h	bool.h	algorithm
bvector.h	defalloc.h	deque.h	deque
faralloc.h	fdeque.h	flist.h	functional
fmap.h	fmultmap.h	fmultset.h	iterator
fset.h	function.h	hdeque.h	list
heap.h	hlist.h	hmap.h	map
hmultmap.h	hmultset.h	hset.h	memory
hugalloc.h	hvector.h	iterator.h	numeric
lbvector.h	ldeque.h	list.h	queue
llist.h	lmap.h	lmultmap.h	set
lmultset.h	lngalloc.h	lset.h	stack
map.h	multimap.h	multiset.h	utility
neralloc.h	nmap.h	nmultmap.h	vector
nmultset.h	nset.h	pair.h	
projectn.h	set.h	stack.h	
tempbuf.h	tree.h	vector.h	

Both VC5 and BC5 conform to the Draft C++ Standard with regard to these headers. If you are using an older compiler (and HP STL), your compiler will probably require *.h* to occur in standard header names, so that you have to write *<vector.h>* and *<iostream.h>* instead of *<vector>* and *<iostream>*. It will then also be necessary to omit *using* statements such as the one that precedes the *main* function in program *readwr.cpp*.

SGI Standard Template Library Adapted for VC++ 5.0

Although VC5 is a very good C++ compiler, there are some problems with the STL version that comes with it. Since they may be solved in the next release of this compiler, we will not discuss them in detail. In the meantime, Visual C++ users should consider downloading a version of STL written by Alexander Stepanov, the designer of STL, for Silicon Graphics (SGI) and adapted for VC5 by Wayne Ouchida. The following web page provides more information about this:

```
http://www.sirius.com/~ouchida/
```

The SGI version of STL is often referred to because of its high quality, and this adaptation enables Visual C++ programmers to benefit from it.

In cases where current STL versions differ, the Draft C++ Standard (of December 1996) is used as a basis for the examples in this book. If you have any portability problems with these when using Microsoft or Borland C++, please refer to the downloadable versions of these programs, available as *stlcpp.zip*. Some of them have been made more portable by using conditional compilation.

There are also commercial STL versions, which we will not discuss here. Since STL consists only of header files, switching from one STL version to another is a simple matter.

1.3 Vectors, Lists and Deques

Program *readwr.cpp* contains three occurrences of the word *vector*:

```
#include <vector>
...
vector<int> v;
...
vector<int>::iterator i;
```

This *vector* concept provides for contiguous memory allocation, for which C programmers traditionally use *malloc*, *realloc* and *free*. Instead, a linked list could be used, as discussed in books on data structures. With STL we can use (doubly) linked lists without programming them ourselves. In program *readwr.cpp*, all we need to do is (consistently) replacing the word *vector* with *list*, as the following program shows:

```
// readwr1.cpp: Reading and writing a variable number of
//    nonzero integers (followed in the input by 0).
//    Based on a list.
#include <iostream>
#include <list>
using namespace std;

int main()
{  list<int> v;
   int x;
   cout << "Enter positive integers, followed by 0:\n";

   while (cin >> x, x != 0)
      v.push_back(x);

   list<int>::iterator i;

   for (i=v.begin(); i != v.end(); ++i)
      cout << *i << " ";
   cout << endl;
   return 0;
}
```

The program is also correct after replacing *list* with *deque*, which gives a third solution. The user will not notice any difference in the behavior of these three program versions, but the internal data representation is different. This is relevant with regard to the available operations that can be performed efficiently.

With a given type *T*, the types *vector<T>*, *deque<T>* and *list<T>* are referred to as *sequence containers*.

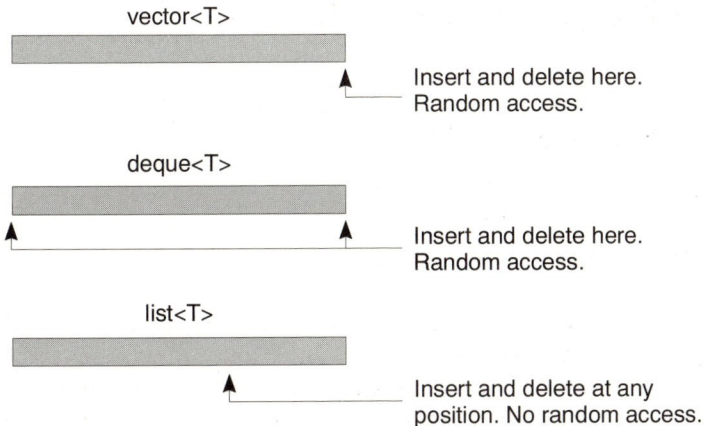

Figure 1.1 *Properties of three sequence containers*

As Figure 1.1 illustrates, we can efficiently insert and delete elements only at the end of a vector, both at the beginning and at the end of a deque and at any position in a list. Although a vector is very limited with regard to insertions and deletions, it has the advantage of providing random access. Some examples will clarify these differences. For the sake of completeness, it should be pointed out that there is a fourth sequence container, the conventional array, defined as

```
T a[N];
```

for an array with elements of type *T*. We will demonstrate that we can successfully use STL to sort an array. In other words, STL can be useful even in programs that use only conventional arrays, not any typical STL container, as we will see in the next section.

As the following table shows, vectors, deques and lists do not support the same set of operations:

Operation	Function	*vector*	*deque*	*list*
insert at the end	*push_back*	✓	✓	✓
delete at the end	*pop_back*	✓	✓	✓
insert at the beginning	*push_front*	-	✓	✓
delete at the beginning	*pop_front*	-	✓	✓
insert anywhere	*insert*	(✓)	(✓)	✓
delete anywhere	*erase*	(✓)	(✓)	✓
sort (see Section 1.4)	*sort* (algorithm)	✓	✓	-

The entry (✓) (in parentheses) indicates that the *insert* and *erase* functions, though available for vectors and deques, are considerably slower for these containers than they are for lists. They are said to be *linear time* for vectors and deques, which means that the time they take is proportional to the length of the sequence stored in the container. By contrast, all operations indicated by ✓ (without parentheses) are *constant time*, that is, the time they require does not depend on the sequence length.

So far, we have only seen the function *push_back* demonstrated. The following program shows how to use all functions (*push_back*, *pop_back*, *push_front*, *pop_front*, *insert* and *erase*) for insertion and deletion, listed in the above table.

```
// insdel.cpp: Insertions and deletions in a list.
#include <iostream>
#include <list>

using namespace std;

void showlist(const char *str, const list<int> &L)
{   list<int>::const_iterator i;
    cout << str << endl << "   ";
    for (i=L.begin(); i != L.end(); ++i)
       cout << *i << " ";
    cout << endl;
}

int main()
{   list<int> L;
    int x;
    cout << "Enter positive integers, followed by 0:\n";
    while (cin >> x, x != 0)
       L.push_back(x);
    showlist("Initial list:", L);
    L.push_front(123);
    showlist("After inserting 123 at the beginning:", L);
    list<int>::iterator i = L.begin();
    L.insert(++i, 456);
    showlist(
       "After inserting 456 at the second position:", L);
    i = L.end();
    L.insert(--i, 999);
    showlist(
       "After inserting 999 just before the end:", L);
    i = L.begin(); x = *i;
    L.pop_front();
    cout << "Deleted at the beginning: " << x << endl;
    showlist("After this deletion:", L);
    i = L.end(); x = *--i;
    L.pop_back();
    cout << "Deleted at the end: " << x << endl;
    showlist("After this deletion:", L);
    i = L.begin();
    x = *++i; cout << "To be deleted: " << x << endl;
    L.erase(i);
```

```
    showlist("After this deletion (of second element):",
       L);
    return 0;
}
```

The functions for insertion and deletion are here applied to a *list*, since this container type is the only one for which all these functions are available and efficient, as the above table indicates. In the following demonstration (and elsewhere in this book), the data entered on the keyboard is underlined:

```
Enter positive integers, followed by 0:
10 20 30    0
Initial list:
  10 20 30
After inserting 123 at the beginning:
  123 10 20 30
After inserting 456 at the second position:
  123 456 10 20 30
After inserting 999 just before the end:
  123 456 10 20 999 30
Deleted at the beginning: 123
After this deletion:
  456 10 20 999 30
Deleted at the end: 30
After this deletion:
  456 10 20 999
To be deleted: 10
After this deletion (of second element):
  456 20 999
```

The occurrences of *const* in the first two lines of the function *showlist* need an explanation:

```
void showlist(const char *str, const list<int> &L)
{  list<int>::const_iterator i;
```

As you probably know, it is good practice to supply pointer and reference parameters with the word *const* in the above way if such parameters do not modify the objects referred to. Since *showlist* modifies neither the string *str* nor the list *L*, there are two occurrences of *const* in the first of these two program lines. Then on the second line we must define the variable *i* as a *const_iterator* to be able to use it for *L*. This is similar to the use of *const* for pointers: if we wanted to assign the above parameter *str* to another pointer, *p*, this would be possible only if we used *const* in the definition of this pointer:

```
const char *p;       // const required because str is
p = str;             // of type const char*
```

Erasing a subsequence

If [*i*1, *i*2) is a valid range in a vector *v*, we can erase the subsequence of *v* given by this range in the following way:

```
v.erase(i1, i2);
```

This also applies to containers other than vector.

1.4 Sorting

The following is an extension of program *readwr.cpp*, discussed at the beginning of Section 1.2. This program sorts vector *v*, that is, it places the elements of *v* in ascending order:

```
// sort1.cpp: Sorting a vector.
#include <iostream>
#include <vector>
#include <algorithm>
using namespace std;

int main()
{   vector<int> v;
    int x;
    cout << "Enter positive integers, followed by 0:\n";
    while (cin >> x, x != 0) v.push_back(x);
    sort(v.begin(), v.end());
    cout << "After sorting: \n";
    vector<int>::iterator i;
    for (i=v.begin(); i != v.end(); ++i)
       cout << *i << " ";
    cout << endl;
    return 0;
}
```

The actual sorting is done by the statement

```
sort(v.begin(), v.end());
```

We use two iterator values as arguments: the first, *v.begin*( ), referring to the initial vector element and the second, *v.end*( ), to the past-the-end element of the vector. The output of this program shows the integers that the user has entered, but in ascending order.

The above call to *sort* is essentially different from calls to *push_back*, *insert*, *begin*, and so on. Since we do not write *v.sort*(...), but simply *sort*(...), we see that *sort* is not a *vector* member function, but a *template function* that is not a class member. The technical term for such STL template functions is *generic algorithm*, or simply *algorithm*. The line

```
#include <algorithm>
```

is required because we use this *sort* algorithm. With some STL implementations, the compiler does not complain if we omit this line because the header *algorithm* is indirectly invoked as a result of the program line

```
#include <vector>
```

Since it would be unwise to count on this, we use both *#include* lines. This is different in the following program, which sorts a normal array instead of a vector:

```
// sort2.cpp: Sorting an array.
#include <iostream>
#include <algorithm>
using namespace std;

int main()
{   int a[10], x, n = 0, *p;
    cout << "Enter at most 10 positive integers, "
        "followed by 0:\n";
    while (cin >> x, x != 0 && n < 10) a[n++] = x;
    sort(a, a+n);
    cout << "After sorting: \n";
    for (p=a; p != a+n; p++) cout << *p << " ";
    cout << endl;
    return 0;
}
```

It is important to note the similarity between the calls

```
sort(v.begin(), v.end());
```

in program *sort1.cpp* and

```
sort(a, a+n);
```

in program *sort2.cpp*. In both calls the first argument refers to the first element of the sequence container and the second to the *past-the-end* element, that is, the position just after the final element. This is a general principle, applying not only to *sort* but to most STL algorithms. We can also apply this principle to a part of a given subsequence. For example, we can sort only $a[3]$, $a[4]$, $a[5]$ and $a[6]$ by writing

```
sort(a+3, a+7);
```

or, equivalently,

```
sort(&a[3], &a[7]);
```

as Figure 1.2 illustrates.

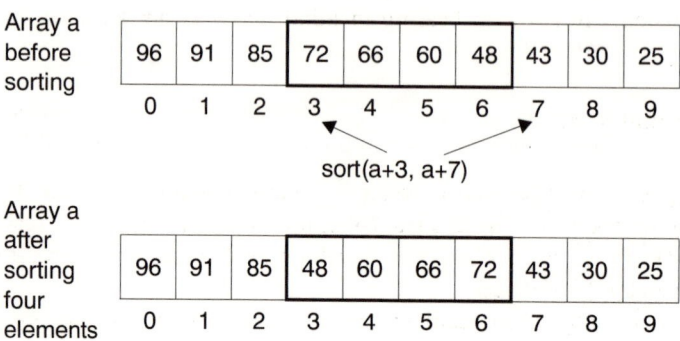

Figure 1.2 *Sorting a subsequence*

It may at first seem more logical to supply the address of the last elements, $a[6]$, instead of that of the past-the-end element, $a[7]$, in this example. However, using the past-the-end element has several advantages. For example, we can now find the number of elements by a simple subtraction:

Number of elements $= 7 - 3 = 4$

This convention also enables us to write the for-loop

```
for (i=3; i!=7; ++i) ...
```

if we want to do something with the sorted elements. The principle of selecting only a subsequence also applies to STL containers, such as vectors. For example, if, in program *sort1.cpp*, vector v also contains at least seven elements, we can sort $v[3]$, $v[4]$, $v[5]$ and $v[6]$ by writing

```
vector<int>::iterator i, j;
i = v.begin() + 3;
j = v.begin() + 7;
sort(i, j);
```

or, simply,

```
sort(v.begin()+3, v.begin()+7);
```

We will discuss this way of using the operator + in more detail in Section 1.9.

Random access, subscripting and sorting

You may wonder why subscripted expressions such as $v[3]$, as occurring in the above discussion, are allowed, bearing in mind that v is not an array but rather defined as

```
vector<int> v;
```

Subscripting is possible because a vector is a random-access container, for which the subscripting operator [ ] is defined. Note, however, that we cannot replace $v[3]$ with $*(v + 3)$, since v has a class type for which neither the binary operator + nor the unary operator * is defined.

The STL *sort* algorithm requires random access. Since this is provided by vectors and arrays, we were able to use this algorithm in the programs *sort1.cpp* and *sort2.cpp*. As Figure 1.1 illustrates, a *deque* also provides random access but a *list* does not. This explains why the call

```
sort(v.begin(), v.end());
```

occurring in program *sort1.cpp*, is also correct if in this program we replace all occurrences of *vector* with *deque*, but it is not if we replace them with *list*. We will discuss this in more detail in Section 1.9.

Initialization of containers

As every C(++) programmer knows, the definition of an array can include a list of initial values. For example, we can write

```
int a[3] = {10, 5, 7};
int b[] = {8, 13};
    // equivalent to int b[2] = {8, 13};
int c[3] = {4};
    // equivalent to int c[3] = {4, 0, 0};
```

Initialization is also possible for the other three types of sequence containers, as this example shows:

```
int a[3] = {10, 5, 7};
vector<int> v(a, a+3);
deque<int> w(a, a+3);
list<int> x(a, a+3);
```

Not only an array but also a vector, a deque or a list can be used as the basis for initializing *the same* container type. For example, if we proceed with

```
vector<int> v1(v.begin(), v.end());
```

vector *v*1 will be identical with vector *v*, both consisting of the three *int* elements 10, 5 and 7. This example is correct because both *v* and *v*1 are of the same container type *vector*. By contrast, the following does not compile, because we cannot use the values of the list *x* to initialize the vector *v*1:

```
vector<int> v1(x.begin(), x.end());
```

It will be clear that this way of initializing is made possible by container class *constructors*. There are also constructors that accept an integer, indicating the desired size and, optionally, a value to be used for all newly created elements. For example, we can write

```
vector<int> v(5, 8); // Five elements, all equal to 8.
```

or

```
vector<int> v(5);
```

In the latter case, the vector *v* has five elements. This form may be useful if we intend to assign values to these elements later, as we will do, for example, in Section 1.6.

1.5 The *find* Algorithm

The following program shows how we can search a vector for a given value:

```
// find1.cpp: Finding a given value in a vector.
#include <iostream>
#include <vector>
#include <algorithm>
using namespace std;

int main()
{   vector<int> v;
    int x;
    cout << "Enter positive integers, followed by 0:\n";
    while (cin >> x, x != 0)
        v.push_back(x);
```

```
   cout << "Value to be searched for: ";
   cin >> x;
   vector<int>::iterator i =
      find(v.begin(), v.end(), x);
   if (i == v.end())
      cout << "Not found\n";
   else
   {  cout << "Found";
      if (i == v.begin())
         cout << " as the first element";
      else cout << " after " << *--i;
   }
   cout << endl;
   return 0;
}
```

The *find* algorithm is applicable to each of the four sequence containers (vector, deque, list and array). If we consistently replace *vector* with *deque*, the program behaves in the same way, and the same applies if we replace *vector* with *list*. The version for an array of *int* values is shown below:

```
// find2.cpp: Finding a given value in an array.

#include <iostream>
#include <algorithm>

using namespace std;

int main()
{  int a[10], x, n = 0;
   cout << "Enter at most 10 positive integers, "
      "followed by 0:\n";
   while (cin >> x, x != 0 && n < 10) a[n++] = x;
   cout << "Value to be searched for: ";
   cin >> x;
   int *p = find(a, a+n, x);
   if (p == a+n)
      cout << "Not found\n";
   else
   {  cout << "Found";
      if (p == a)
         cout << " as the first element";
      else cout << " after " << *--p;
   }
   cout << endl;
   return 0;
}
```

1.6 The *copy* Algorithm and an Insert Iterator

We can use the *copy* algorithm to copy the elements of one container to another, where, for example, the source can be a vector and the destination a list, as the following program illustrates:

```
// copy1.cpp: Copying a vector to a list.
//            First version: overwrite mode.
#include <iostream>
#include <vector>
#include <list>
using namespace std;

int main()
{  int a[4] = {10, 20, 30, 40};
   vector<int> v(a, a+4);
   list<int> L(4);  // A list of 4 elements
   copy(v.begin(), v.end(), L.begin());
   list<int>::iterator i;
   for (i=L.begin(); i != L.end(); ++i)
      cout << *i << " "; // Output: 10 20 30 40
   cout << endl;
   return 0;
}
```

Overwrite and insert modes

Since four elements are to be copied to the list *L*, it is given the length 4 in its definition

```
list<int> L(4);  // A list of 4 elements
```

This is required here because the *copy* algorithm, when used in this way, works in *overwrite mode*. This is similar to the way characters can be entered on the keyboard with a text processor in overwrite mode. When typing in this way, we overwrite existing text; most users will therefore prefer the *insert mode*. On a normal keyboard, the *Ins* key switches from insert mode to overwrite mode, and vice versa. As for the *copy* algorithm, it is not difficult to switch to insert mode either. First, we begin with an empty list, replacing the above definition of *L* with the following one:

```
list<int> L;     // An empty list.
```

Then we replace the call to the *copy* algorithm with this one:

```
copy(v.begin(), v.end(), inserter(L, L.begin()));
```

With these two program modifications, list *L* will obtain the same contents as in the original program. The new form

```
inserter(...)
```

is technically known as an *insert iterator*, which is a special form of an *iterator adaptor*, as we will see in Section 6.6. We can also use it to insert some data in the middle of a sequence, as the following version shows:

```
// copy2.cpp: Copying a vector to a list.
//             Second version: insert mode.

#include <iostream>
#include <vector>
#include <list>

using namespace std;

int main()
{   int a[4] = {10, 20, 30, 40};
    vector<int> v(a, a+4);
    list<int> L(5, 123);   // A list of 5 elements
    list<int>::iterator i = L.begin();
    ++i;
    ++i;
    copy(v.begin(), v.end(), inserter(L, i));
    for (i=L.begin(); i != L.end(); ++i)
       cout << *i << " ";
    cout << endl;
    return 0;
}
```

The initial contents of the list *L* is as follows:

```
123 123 123 123 123
```

Then iterator *i* is made to refer to the third element of this list, after which it is used in the expression

```
inserter(L, i)
```

which occurs in the call to *copy*. This causes the values 10, 20, 30 and 40 to be inserted at the third element of the list, shifting this third element and its successors four positions to the right. This explains the following output of this program:

```
123 123 10 20 30 40 123 123 123
```

Output and input

Curiously enough, we can also use the *copy* algorithm for output and input, as we will see in Section 1.9.

1.7 The *merge* Algorithm

Figure 1.3 illustrates the *merge* operation. Two ordered sequences are combined into one, giving a new ordered sequence.

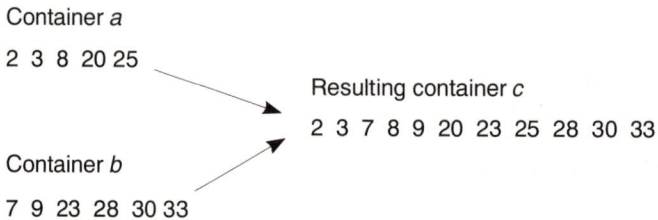

Figure 1.3 *Merging* **a** *and* **b** *into* **c**

The *merge* algorithm can be used for each of the four sequence container types (arrays, vectors, deques and lists). Surprisingly, the three participants (*a*, *b* and *c* in Figure 1.3) need not belong to the same container type. To demonstrate this, let us merge vector *a* and array *b* into list *c*:

```
// merge.cpp: Merging a vector and an array into a list.
#include <iostream>
#include <vector>
#include <list>
#include <algorithm>
using namespace std;

int main()
{  vector<int> a(5);
   a[0] = 2; a[1] = 3; a[2] = 8;
   a[3] = 20; a[4] = 25;
   int b[6] = {7, 9, 23, 28, 30, 33};
   list<int> c; // List c is initially empty
   merge(a.begin(), a.end(), b, b+6,
      inserter(c, c.begin()));
   list<int>::iterator i;
   for (i=c.begin(); i != c.end(); ++i)
      cout << *i << " ";
   cout << endl;
   return 0;
}
```

As with *copy*, we have to use an inserter iterator if we want to write into list *c* in insert mode. Alternatively, we could have written

```
list<int> c(11); // destination: 5 + 6 = 11 elements
merge(a.begin(), a.end(), b, b+6, c.begin());
```

allocating enough room in the destination *c* in its definition. The *merge* algorithm itself works in overwrite mode, that is, it does not generate any new container elements but it puts values in existing ones. To insert new elements during the merge process we have to use the inserter iterator as shown in the complete program. Either way, the program produces the following output:

```
2  3  7  8  9  20  23  25  28  30  33
```

As in Section 1.4, we have applied subscripting, writing, for example, $a[0]$, although *a* is a vector, not an array. This array notation is also possible for deques, but not for lists. Recall that lists are also different from arrays, vectors and deques in that we cannot apply the sort algorithm to them, as we have seen in Section 1.4. We will return to this subject in Section 1.9.

1.8 User-defined Types

So far, the containers we have been using had elements of type *int*. Besides standard types, such as *int*, user-defined types are also suitable element types for STL containers. Since the call *merge(...)* in program *merge.cpp* is based on the less-than operator <, a similar call for these new types will be possible only if we define the operator < for these types. Let us demonstrate this for a simple case:

```
// merge2.cpp: Merging records, with names as keys.

#include <iostream>
#include <string>
#include <algorithm>

using namespace std;

struct entry {
   long nr;
   char name[30];
   bool operator<(const entry &b)const
   {  return strcmp(name, b.name) < 0;
   }
};
```

```
int main()
{  entry a[3] = {{10, "Betty"},
                 {11, "James"},
                 {80, "Jim"}},
         b[2] = {{16, "Fred"},
                 {20, "William"}},
         c[5], *p;
   merge(a, a+3, b, b+2, c);
   for (p=c; p != c+5; p++)
      cout << p->nr << " " << p->name << endl;
   cout << endl;
   return 0;
}
```

It is essential that the names in each of the arrays a and b appear in alphabetic order. The program merges a and b into c (according to the alphabetic order of the names) as the following output illustrates:

```
10 Betty
16 Fred
11 James
80 Jim
20 William
```

If, instead, we want the numbers to appear in ascending order, we have to list them in that order in the given arrays a and b, and we also have to replace the less-than operator. Since the numbers already happen to be in ascending order in both arrays, we only have to replace the current *operator<* member function with the following one:

```
bool operator<(const entry &b)const
{  return nr < b.nr;
}
```

After this program modification, the numbers appear in ascending order in the output:

```
10 Betty
11 James
16 Fred
20 William
80 Jim
```

The *operator<* function need not be a member of class *entry*. In other words, we could have written

```
struct entry {
   long nr;
   char name[30];
};

bool operator<(const entry &a, const entry &b)
{  return strcmp(a.name, b.name) < 0;
}
```

instead of the definition of class *entry* as this occurs in program *merge2.cpp*. Incidentally, we will see in Section 7.3.7 that there is also a version of *merge* that allows us to specify a comparison function as an argument.

1.9 Iterator Categories

As we have seen in Section 1.4, we can apply the *sort* algorithm to arrays, to vectors and to deques, but not to lists. By contrast, the *find* algorithm can be applied to all these four container types. (In this section, we are using the term *container* for what is actually a *sequence container*, ignoring other container types to be discussed in Chapters 2 and 4.) It will be clear that we only need one pass over all elements to find a given value, while efficient sorting requires random access. In both cases *iterators* are used, but the *sort* algorithm requires 'more powerful' iterators than does the *find* algorithm. It makes sense to divide iterators into five categories, according to the operations that are defined for them. Suppose that i and j are iterators of the same type. Then the three operations

```
i == j          i != j          i = j
```

are possible, regardless of the iterator category. As for some other operations, the following table shows which apply to each iterator category; we suppose that x is a variable of the same type as the container elements in question and that n is of type *int*:

Iterator category	Operations (in addition to $i == j, i != j, i = j$)	Provided by containers	Required by typical algorithm
input	$x = *i, ++i, i++$	all four	*find*
output	$*i = x, ++i, i++$	all four	*copy* (destination)
forward	as both input and output	all four	*replace*
bidirectional	as forward and $--i, i--$	all four	*reverse*
random access	as bidirectional and $i + n, i - n,$ $i += n, i -= n,$ $i < j, i > j, i <= j, i >= j$	*array,* *vector,* *deque* (not *list*)	*sort*

According to the second column of this table, a *forward* iterator provides all operations of *input* iterators and all those of *output* iterators. *Bidirectional* iterators provide pre- and post-decrement operations in addition to all operations provided by forward iterators. Adding yet another set of operations (+, −, +=, −=, <, >, <= and >=), we arrive at the *random-access* iterator category. Adding an integer to an iterator is possible only for random-access iterators; this operation is required, for example, by the *sort* algorithm. Since a *list* does not provide a random-access iterator, we cannot apply the *sort* algorithm to a list.

Program *find*1 in Section 1.5 contains the line

```
else cout << " after " << *--i;
```

You may have wondered why we did not use the expression $*(i-1)$ instead of $*--i$; after all, it is not necessary to change the value of i. We are now in a position to see that $i-1$ is valid only for random-access iterators, while $--i$ is also correct for bidirectional iterators. In its current form, program *find*1 is based on a vector, and since a vector provides the random-access iterator category, the form $*(i-1)$ would not have caused any problem. It would, however, if the word *vector* is consistently replaced with the word *list* in this program. In that case, i would have been a bidirectional iterator, for which the expression $i-1$ is not valid. In other words, program *find*1 no longer compiles if, at the same time, we replace *vector* with *list* and $*--i$ with $*(i-1)$. Neither is the less-than operator available for iterators provided by lists. The comments in the following fragment illustrate this:

```
// Demonstration of random-access iterators:
int a[3] = {5, 8, 2};
vector<int> v(a, a+3);
vector<int>::iterator iv = v.begin(), iv1;

iv1 = iv + 1;
bool b1 = iv < iv1;
// In the last two lines, + and < are allowed
// because iv and iv1 are random-access iterators.


// Demonstration of bidirectional iterators:
list<int> w(a, a+3);
list<int>::iterator iw = w.begin(), iw1;

iw1 = iw + 1;           // Error
bool b2 = iw < iw1;     // Error
// In the last two lines, + and < are not allowed
// because iw and iw1 are bidirectional iterators.
// By contrast, the following two lines are correct:
iw1 = iw;
bool b3 = iw == iw1;
```

Iterator category required by algorithms

Of all possible operations on iterators, the *find* algorithm (discussed in Section 1.5) only requires those which are provided by input iterators, since it needs only to 'read' sequence elements, executing, for example, the assignment $x = {*}i$. This is why the name *find* occurs as an example for input iterators in the column *Required by typical algorithm* of the above table.

Recall that we used the *copy* algorithm (also listed in the above table) as follows in Section 1.6:

```
copy(v.begin(), v.end(), L.begin());
```

To verify that this is in accordance with the above table, observe that the destination L is a *list*, which provides the bidirectional iterator category. Only the output-iterator category is required for L, but bidirectional iterators support all output-iterator operations, so there is no problem. Since the *copy* algorithm requires only an output iterator as its third argument, it will not apply the operators $--, +, -, <, <=, >=$ and $>$ to iterators referring to elements of L; neither will it 'read' anything from L by executing something like $x = {*}i$. The opposite operation, ${*}i = x$, will be executed, however, to 'write' the copied values into L.

Stream iterators: using *copy* for input and output

We can use the *copy* algorithm to perform output, as the following fragment illustrates:

```
const int N = 4;
int a[N] = {7, 6, 9, 2};
copy(a, a+N, ostream_iterator<int>(cout, " "));
```

We can also define an iterator variable i to use this as the third argument of copy. This is done by replacing the above call to *copy* with these two statements:

```
ostream_iterator<int> i(cout, " ");
copy(a, a+N, i);
```

In either case, the numbers 7, 6, 9 and 2 are written to *cout*, as if we had written

```
for (int* p=a; p != a+N; p++)
   cout << *p << " ";
```

We can use the same idea for input, writing

```
istream_iterator<int, ptrdiff_t>(file)
```

where *file* is the input stream. This rather complex expression is to be used instead of, for example, *v.begin*( ), which we would use if we wanted to copy from the container *v*. If we omit *file* on the above line, we obtain the expression

```
istream_iterator<int, ptrdiff_t>()
```

to be used instead of *v.end*( ) because it denotes end-of-file. For example, suppose that we are given the file *example.txt*, with the following contents:

```
10  20  30
40  50
```

It is given that this file contains only integers (separated and possibly followed by white-space characters), but we do not know how many integers there are in the file. The following program reads the integers from this file and displays them on the screen; conditional compilation is used here so that the program is also accepted by BC5, which requires a second argument for the *istream_iterator* constructor:

```
// copyio.cpp: Using the copy algorithm for I/O.

#include <fstream>
#include <iostream>
#include <iterator>
#include <vector>
using namespace std;

#ifdef __BORLANDC__   // Tested with BC5.2
typedef istream_iterator<int, ptrdiff_t> istream_iter;
#else
typedef istream_iterator<int> istream_iter;
#endif

int main()
{  vector<int> a;
   ifstream file("example.txt");
   if (file.fail())
   {  cout << "Cannot open file example.txt.\n";
      return 1;
   }
   copy(istream_iter(file), istream_iter(),
      inserter(a, a.begin()));
   copy(a.begin(), a.end(),
      ostream_iterator<int>(cout, " "));
   cout << endl;
   return 0;
}
```

Since the program ignores the structure of the input file, its output consists of only one line:

```
10 20 30 40 50
```

We will return to the subject of stream iterators in Section 6.6.

Iterator operations

Recall that we can perform arithmetic operations with random-access iterators in the same way as we can with pointers, writing, for example,

```
int n, dist;
...   // i and i0 are random-access iterators
i0 = i;
i += n;
dist = i - i0;  // dist == n
```

Instead, we can use the functions *advance* and *distance*, as the following fragment shows:

```
int n, dist;
...   // i and i0 are iterators, not necessarily
      // belonging to the random-access category
i0 = i;
advance(i, n);
distance(i0, i, dist);  // dist == n
```

This works for all iterators, provided the value of n is reasonable, so that the modified value of i refers either to an existing element of the container in question or to the past-the-end element. If i is a forward iterator, n can only be positive. Then the above call to *advance* has the same effect as applying the ++ operator n times to i. The *advance* and *distance* operations will be executed much faster for random-access iterators than for other iterator types.

1.10 The *replace* and *reverse* Algorithms

The *replace* algorithm, listed in the table of Section 1.9, enables us, for a given container, to find all its elements that have a given value and to replace these with another value. The following program illustrates this:

```
// replace.cpp: Replacing sequence elements.
#include <iostream>
#include <string>
#include <algorithm>
using namespace std;
```

```
int main()
{   char str[] = "abcabcabc";
    int n = strlen(str);
    replace(str, str+n, 'b', 'q');
    cout << str << endl;
    return 0;
}
```

In *str*, all elements equal to '*b*' are replaced with '*q*', so this program produces the following output:

```
aqcaqcaqc
```

The *reverse* algorithm, also mentioned in the table of Section 1.9, makes it easy to replace a sequence with its reverse. According to the table, it requires bidirectional iterators, which, as we know, are provided by all four sequence containers. Let us demonstrate this algorithm by using an array again.

```
// reverse.cpp: Replacing a string with its reverse.
#include <iostream>
#include <string>
#include <algorithm>

using namespace std;

int main()
{   char str[] = "abcklmxyz";
    reverse(str, str+strlen(str));
    cout << str << endl;   // Output: zyxmlkcba
    return 0;
}
```

1.11 The *sort* Algorithm Revisited

The C standard library function *qsort* is very general, since it takes a user-defined compare function as its fourth argument. We have seen no such thing in Section 1.4, when we were using the *sort* algorithm, so you may expect sort to rely completely on the meaning of the less-than operator <. When dealing with arrays of class objects, we can give this operator any meaning we like, but this is not possible if the array elements are of some built-in type, such as *int*. Suppose we want an array to be sorted in descending rather than in ascending order. Of course we could do this by first sorting the array in ascending order and then applying the *reverse* algorithm, discussed in the previous section. Instead, we can do this by supplying the *sort* algorithm with a third argument, which, as with *qsort*, is a compare function. The following program demonstrates this:

```
// dsort1.cpp: Sorting in descending order,
//    using a compare function.
#include <iostream>
#include <algorithm>
using namespace std;

bool comparefun(int x, int y)
{  return x > y;
}

int main()
{  const int N = 8;
   int a[N] =
       {1234, 5432, 8943, 3346, 9831, 7842, 8863, 9820};
   cout << "Before sorting:\n";
   copy(a, a+N, ostream_iterator<int>(cout, " "));
   cout << endl;
   sort(a, a+N, comparefun);
   cout << "After sorting in descending order:\n";
   copy(a, a+N, ostream_iterator<int>(cout, " "));
   cout << endl;
   return 0;
}
```

Recall that we have discussed the above use of *copy* at the end of Section 1.9.

We have to define the function *comparefun* in such a way that the value of *comparefun(a[i], a[j])* is *true* if and only if, after sorting, $a[i]$ is to precede $a[j]$. Functions such as *comparefun*, returning a *bool* value, are called *predicates*.

The program produces the following output:

```
Before sorting:
1234 5432 8943 3346 9831 7842 8863 9820
After sorting in descending order:
9831 9820 8943 8863 7842 5432 3346 1234
```

1.12 Introduction to Function Objects

There is a different way of solving the sorting problem of the previous section. Although we do not really need it for this problem, the principle we will be discussing is very important in more complex situations, so it would not be wise to skip this section. A *function object* is a class in which the call operator, written *operator( )*, is defined. There need not be any other class members. Let us begin with a very simple example. (Here and elsewhere we write *iostream.h* instead of *iostream* because, with the latter, VC5 also requires the *using namespace std* line, while BC5 complains about this if no typical STL header, such as *vector*, is used.)

```
// funobj.cpp: A very simple function object.

#include <iostream.h>

class compare {
public:
   int operator()(int x, int y)const
   {  return x > y;
   }
};

int main()
{  compare v;
   cout << v(2, 15) << endl;          // Output: 0
   cout << compare()(5, 3) << endl; // Output: 1
   cout << endl;
   return 0;
}
```

Since a function call, *operator*(), with two *int* parameters, is defined for class *compare*, we can write the expression *v*(2, 15) where *v* is a variable of this class. This expression is actually an abbreviated form of *v.operator*()(2, 15), so it causes the member function *operator*() of class *compare* to be called, resulting in the value 0 because 2 is not greater than 15. The second call

```
compare()(5, 3)
```

has a rather unusual appearance. Its first part, *compare*(), is a call to the default constructor of class *compare*. In other words, the expression *compare*() represents an object of type *compare*, and, like *v*, it can therefore be followed by an argument list, such as (5, 3).

The following program, based on a function object, is equivalent to *dsort*1 of the previous section:

```
// dsort2.cpp: Sorting in descending order,
//    using a function object of our own.

#include <iostream>
#include <algorithm>

using namespace std;

class compare {
public:
   bool operator()(int x, int y)const
   {  return x > y;
   }
};
```

```
int main()
{   const int N = 8;
    int a[N] =
        {1234, 5432, 8943, 3346, 9831, 7842, 8863, 9820};
    cout << "Before sorting:\n";
    copy(a, a+N, ostream_iterator<int>(cout, " "));
    cout << endl;
    sort(a, a+N, compare());
    cout << "After sorting in descending order:\n";
    copy(a, a+N, ostream_iterator<int>(cout, " "));
    cout << endl;
    return 0;
}
```

It is not really necessary to define the class *compare*, since STL includes such a definition, in the more general form of a template. We can therefore simply omit the class *compare* and, in the call to the *sort* algorithm, replace *compare*() with *greater<int>*(). This results in the following, final version:

```
// dsort3.cpp: Sorting in descending order,
//      using the 'greater' template.
#include <iostream>
#include <algorithm>
#include <functional>
using namespace std;

int main()
{   const int N = 8;
    int a[N] =
        {1234, 5432, 8943, 3346, 9831, 7842, 8863, 9820};
    cout << "Before sorting:\n";
    copy(a, a+N, ostream_iterator<int>(cout, " "));
    cout << endl;
    sort(a, a+N, greater<int>());
    cout << "After sorting in descending order:\n";
    copy(a, a+N, ostream_iterator<int>(cout, " "));
    cout << endl;
    return 0;
}
```

We will discuss function objects in more detail in Chapter 6.

1.13 Using *find_if*, *remove* and *remove_if*

In this section we will discuss three algorithms, using them for vectors but bearing in mind that they also apply to deques and lists.

The *find_if* algorithm

In addition to the *find* algorithm, which we used in Section 1.5 to find vector elements of a given value, there is also the *find_if* algorithm, which is more general in that it takes a predicate (see Section 1.11) as an argument. It searches the vector for the first element that satisfies the condition specified by that predicate. For example, the following program searches a vector for the first element *i satisfying

$$3 \leq *i \leq 8$$

The program tests whether such an element is found, and displays its value if this is the case:

```cpp
// find_if.cpp: The find_if algorithm demonstrated.

#include <iostream>
#include <vector>
#include <algorithm>

using namespace std;

bool condition(int x)
{   return 3 <= x && x <= 8;
}

int main()
{   vector<int> v;
    v.push_back(10);
    v.push_back(7);
    v.push_back(4);
    v.push_back(1);
    vector<int>::iterator i;
    i = find_if(v.begin(), v.end(), condition);
    if (i != v.end())
        cout << "Found element: " << *i << endl;
    return 0;
}
```

As you will expect, the output of this program is

```
Found element: 7
```

because, in {10, 7, 4, 1}, the value 7 is the first to lie between 3 and 8. This program also works correctly if we use a function object (see Section 1.12) instead of a function. If we want to do this, we can replace the above function *condition* with this class definition:

```
class CondObject {
public:
   bool operator()(int x)
   {  return 3 <= x && x <= 8;
   }
};
```

At the same time, we replace the above call to *find_if* with the following one:

```
i = find_if(v.begin(), v.end(), CondObject());
```

The *remove* and *remove_if* algorithms

Suppose we want to delete all vector elements that are equal to a given value. We could do this by using the *find* and *erase* functions repeatedly, but there is a far more efficient way to obtain the same result. We need to perform two steps:

1. Rearranging the vector by a call to *remove*, to place all elements that we want to retain at the beginning of the vector. This process is *stable*: the order in which the retained elements occur is the same as the original one.

2. Erasing all elements that we do not want to retain; these are now at the end of the vector.

The *remove* algorithms returns the logical new end, without changing the size of the container. We can then erase the 'garbage' elements by starting at the returned new end, using the *erase* member function, discussed at the end of Section 1.3. The following program illustrates this by removing all elements equal to 1 from a sequence:

```
// remove.cpp: The remove algorithm.

#include <iostream>
#include <vector>
#include <algorithm>
#include <iterator>

using namespace std;

void out(const char *s, const vector<int> &v)
{  cout << s;
   copy(v.begin(), v.end(),
      ostream_iterator<int>(cout, " "));
   cout << endl;
}
```

```
int main()
{   vector<int> v;
    vector<int>::iterator new_end;
    v.push_back(1); v.push_back(4); v.push_back(1);
    v.push_back(3); v.push_back(1); v.push_back(2);
    out("Initial sequence v:\n", v);
    new_end = remove(v.begin(), v.end(), 1);
    out("After new_end = remove(v.begin(), "
        "v.end(), 1):\n", v);
    v.erase(new_end, v.end());
    out("After v.erase(new_end, v.end()):\n", v);
    return 0;
}
```

Starting with the sequence {1, 4, 1, 3, 1, 2}, this program logically removes the elements equal to 1; the remaining elements are placed in the first

$$new\_end - v.begin = 3$$

elements, where *new_end* is the value returned by the call to *remove*. The other three elements, starting at position *new_end*, are then erased by the *erase* member function. The output of this program is shown below:

```
Initial sequence v:
1 4 1 3 1 2
After new_end = remove(v.begin(), v.end(), 1):
4 3 2 3 1 2
After v.erase(new_end, v.end()):
4 3 2
```

The *stability* of the *remove* algorithm is illustrated by the order 4, 3, 2 of the resulting elements; this order is the same as that in which these values occurred in the initial sequence. Although the *remove* algorithm is also available for lists, there is also a list member function *remove*, which is to be preferred, as we will see in Section 3.5.

There is also an algorithm *remove_if*, which is a generalize version of *remove*, in the same way as *find_if* is a generalization of *find*. The following program shows how we can use the *remove_if* algorithm, again combined with the *erase* member function, to erase all elements less than or equal to 2:

```
// rm_if.cpp: The remove_if algorithm.

#include <iostream>
#include <vector>
#include <algorithm>
#include <iterator>
```

```
using namespace std;

void out(const char *s, const vector<int> &v)
{   cout << s;
    copy(v.begin(), v.end(),
        ostream_iterator<int>(cout, " "));
    cout << endl;
}

bool cond(int x)
{   return x <= 2;
}

int main()
{   vector<int> v;
    vector<int>::iterator new_end;
    v.push_back(1); v.push_back(4); v.push_back(1);
    v.push_back(3); v.push_back(1); v.push_back(2);
    out("Initial sequence v:\n", v);
    new_end = remove_if(v.begin(), v.end(), cond);
    v.erase(new_end, v.end());
    out("After erasing all elements <= 2:\n", v);
    return 0;
}
```

This program produces the following output:

```
Initial sequence v:
1 4 1 3 1 2
After erasing all elements <= 2:
4 3
```

As *remove*, the *remove_if* algorithm is stable, so it is no coincidence that the order of 4 and 3 in the result is the same as it was in the initial sequence.

1.14 The *auto_ptr* Class

After we have allocated memory we must be very careful to deallocate it correctly. Traditionally, C programmers use *malloc* and *free* for this purpose, while C++ programmers also use *new* and *delete*. The first thing to remember is that after

```
int *p = new int;
int *q = new int[n];
```

we normally have to execute the following statements later:

```
delete p;
delete[] q;
```

The placement of the bracket pair [ ] for *q* but not for *p* is a very common source of errors. Another difficulty is that we must be careful with copies to pointers. For example, if we write

```
int *a = new int[n], *b;
b = a;
```

the pointers *a* and *b* point to the same memory block. Deallocating this block must be done exactly once, so that later we should execute either

```
delete[] a;
```

or

```
delete[] b;
```

but not both.

There is a special class, *auto_ptr*, which makes it safer to use the *new* operator in complex situations. The member function *get* returns the pointer that actually points to the data. If we assign the *auto_ptr* object *a* to the variable *b*, the pointer *a.get*( ) is automatically set to *NULL*, as the following program shows:

```
// auto_ptr.cpp: Data is pointed to only once.

#include <iostream>
#include <memory>

using namespace std;

int main()
{   auto_ptr<int> a(new int), b;
    *a.get() = 123;
    cout << "*a.get() = " << *a.get() << endl;
    b = a;
    cout << "The assignment b = a has been executed.\n";
    if (a.get() == NULL)
        cout << "As a result, a.get() is NULL.\n";
    cout << "*b.get() = " << *b.get() << endl;
    return 0;
}
```

This program produces the following output:

```
*a.get() = 123
The assignment b = a has been executed.
As a result, a.get() is NULL.
*b.get() = 123
```

Since *a.get*( ) is a (normal) pointer, the value pointed to is denoted by **a.get*( ). The advantage of this *auto_ptr* class is that memory deallocation takes place automatically when the class object is destroyed, and this is done only once: in our example, the variables *a* and *b* do not both contain a pointer to the same memory location. To make this clear, let us have a look at the *auto_ptr* destructor, where *the_p* is the private data member pointing to the data in question:

```
~auto_ptr(){delete the_p;}
```

In our program, this destructor is executed for both *a* and *b*, so that the two actions

```
delete a.the_p;
delete b.the_p;
```

take place, which seems to be wrong. However, one of the two pointers used here is equal to *NULL*, and applying *delete* to a pointer equal to *NULL* is allowed and has no effect.

It should be mentioned that there is a unary operator * returning **the_p*. Since the member function *get* returns the pointer *the_p*, the notation we have been using could have been more compact. For example, instead of

```
*a.get() = 123;
```

we can simply write

```
*a = 123;
```

but we should be aware that *a* is not a real pointer.

Warning

Unlike most other STL facilities, the *auto_ptr* class is sometimes accused of weird behavior, so you should use it only if you know exactly what you are doing. For example, after the execution of

```
auto_ptr<int> a(new int), b;
*a.get() = 123;
b = a;
```

we will at first find it very strange that, while **b* is well defined and equal to 123, we cannot use the expression **a* because the last assignment makes the actual *int* pointer contained in *a* equal to *NULL*. As we have seen, the reason for this is that the memory allocated by the *new* operator will automatically be deallocated exactly once.

2

More Algorithms and Containers

2.1 The *accumulate* Algorithm

Forming the sum of all (or of some contiguous) elements of a sequence is best done by using the *accumulate* algorithm. This algorithm and some others, also related to numerical computations, are defined in the header *numeric*, not in *algorithm* as are most others. (If you are working with HP STL, you should use *algo.h*, not *algorithm* or *numeric*.) The following program shows how to apply this *accumulate* algorithm to an array:

```
// accum1.cpp: Forming sums.
#include <iostream>
#include <numeric>
using namespace std;

int main()
{   const int N = 8;
    int a[N] = {4, 12, 3, 6, 10, 7, 8, 5}, sum = 0;
    sum = accumulate(a, a+N, sum);
    cout << "Sum of all elements: " << sum << endl;
    cout << "1000 + a[2] + a[3] + a[4] = "
         << accumulate(a+2, a+5, 1000) << endl;
    return 0;
}
```

The first and second arguments of *accumulate* indicate the sequence of which we want to compute the sum. The third argument is the initial value in the summation process, and will therefore normally be equal to zero. In the first call to accumulate, we could have used the constant 0 instead of the variable *sum* as this third argument. Here is a demonstration of this program:

```
Sum of all elements: 55
1000 + a[2] + a[3] + a[4] = 1019
```

The displayed values are computed as

$$0 + 4 + 12 + 3 + 6 + 10 + 7 + 8 + 5 = 55$$
$$1000 + 3 + 6 + 10 = 1019$$

The template *multiplies<int>*( ) is similar to *greater<int>*( ) discussed at the end of Section 1.12. We can use it if we want a product rather than a sum:

```
// accum2.cpp: Forming a product.
#include <iostream>
#include <numeric>
#include <algorithm>
#include <functional>
using namespace std;

int main()
{   const int N = 4;
    int a[N] = {2, 10, 5, 3}, prod = 1;
    prod = accumulate(a, a+N, prod, multiplies<int>());
    // ('multiplies' has replaced 'times')
    cout << "Product of all elements: " << prod << endl;
    return 0;
}
```

Note that originally the name *times* had to be used instead of *multiplies*. This is still the case with BC 5.2. The output of this program consists of the value 300 (= $1 \times 2 \times 10 \times 5 \times 3$). It is essential in this case that the third argument should be 1 (which is the 'identity' or 'neutral' element for multiplication). The fourth argument indicates that integer multiplication is to take place.

We will now use the *accumulate* algorithm once again, but this time supplying a function object of our own. With a given array *a* of, say, four elements the following value is computed:

```
1 * a[0] + 2 * a[1] + 4 * a[2] + 8 * a[3]
```

Besides a function *operator*( ), our function object now also contains both an *int* data member, used for the successive powers 1, 2, 4 and 8, and a constructor to initialize this data member:

```
// accum3.cpp: Forming the following sum:
//    1 * a[0] + 2 * a[1] + 4 * a[2] + 8 * a[3].

#include <iostream>
#include <numeric>

using namespace std;

class fun {
public:
   fun(){i = 1;}
   int operator()(int x, int y)
   {  int u = x + i * y;
      i *= 2;
      return u;
   }
private:
   int i;
};

int main()
{  const int N = 4;
   int a[N] = {7, 6, 9, 2}, prod = 0;
   prod = accumulate(a, a+N, prod, fun());
   cout << prod << endl;
   return 0;
}
```

The output of this program is the value 71 (= $1 \times 7 + 2 \times 6 + 4 \times 9 + 8 \times 2$).

2.2 The *for_each* Algorithm

We can use the *for_each* algorithm to apply a function to each element of a sequence. Here is a program to demonstrate this:

```
// for_each.cpp: The for_each algorithm.

#include <iostream>
#include <algorithm>

using namespace std;

void display(int x)
{  static int i=0;
   cout << "a[" << i++ << "] = " << x << endl;
}
```

```
int main()
{   const int N = 4;
    int a[N] =
        {1234, 5432, 8943, 3346};
    for_each(a, a+N, display);
    return 0;
}
```

This program works in the same way as it would if we replaced the above call to *for_each* with this for-statement:

```
for (int *p=a; p != a+N; p++)
    display(*p);
```

In either case, it gives the following output:

```
a[0] = 1234
a[1] = 5432
a[2] = 8943
a[3] = 3346
```

The function *display* in this example has a serious drawback: the variable i is equal to zero only the very first time this function is called. For example, writing another, identical call to *for_each* in the *main* function would be a serious error because *display* would not start with $i = 0$ in the second call. We can solve this problem by using a function object. We replace the function *display* with the following class definition:

```
class display {
public:
    display(): i(0){}
    void operator()(int x)
    {   cout << "a[" << i++ << "] = " << x << endl;
    }
private:
    int i;
};
```

We also add a pair of parentheses in the third argument of *for_each*:

```
for_each(a, a+N, display());
```

With these changes, the program produces the same output. Unlike the original program, it simply produces this output twice if we write two such *for_each* calls.

2.3 Counting

The *count* algorithm counts how many elements of a sequence are equal to a given value. Let us apply it to a string, counting how often, say, the letter *e* occurs in it:

```
// count_e.cpp: Counting how often 'e' occurs.
#include <iostream>
#include <string>
#include <algorithm>
using namespace std;

int main() // Change required for BC5.2 (see below).
{  char *p =
      "This demonstrates the Standard Template Library";
   int n = count(p, p + strlen(p), 'e');
   cout << n << " occurrences of 'e' found.\n";
   return 0;
}
```

In the original STL version, the *count* algorithm did not return a value but used a fourth parameter, which was increased by the count value. This is still the case with BC 5.2.

The following program counts how often characters belonging to the set {*'a'*, *'e'*, *'i'*, *'o'*, *'u'*} (also known as *vowels*) occur in the given string.

```
// countvw1.cpp: Count how often the vowels
//      a, e, i, o, u occur in a given string.
//      (initial version).
#include <iostream>
#include <string>
#include <algorithm>
using namespace std;

int main() // See also count_e.cpp.
{  char *p =
      "This demonstrates the Standard Template Library",
      *q = p + strlen(p);
   int n = count(p, q, 'a') +
      count(p, q, 'e') +
      count(p, q, 'i') +
      count(p, q, 'o') +
      count(p, q, 'u');
   cout << n << " vowels (a, e, i, o, u) found.\n";
      // n = 13
   return 0;
}
```

Unfortunately, this approach is not particularly efficient, since the given string is scanned five times while we would prefer a single scan. This is possible by using the *count_if* algorithm, in which we can supply a function to determine whether the condition in question is satisfied. The number of parameters of *count_if* has recently been reduced by 1, in the same way as with *count*.

```
// countvw2.cpp: Count how often the vowels
//    a, e, i, o, u occur in a given string
//    (improved version).
#include <iostream>
#include <string>
#include <algorithm>
using namespace std;

bool found(char ch)
{  return ch == 'a' || ch == 'e' || ch == 'i' ||
           ch == 'o' || ch == 'u';
}

int main() // BC5.2 requires a modification.
{  char *p =
        "This demonstrates the Standard Template Library";
    int n = count_if(p, p + strlen(p), found);
    cout << n << " vowels (a, e, i, o, u) found.\n";
        // n = 13
    return 0;
}
```

2.4 STL-Provided Function Objects

Remember that functions such as *found* in the previous section are called *predicates*. They return *true* or *false* indicating whether some condition is satisfied. The expression *greater<int>()*, occurring in Section 1.11, is another predicate, but this one is a template, provided by STL. Recall that, to sort a sequence in descending order, we used it in the call

```
sort(a, a+N, greater<int>());
```

In Section 2.1 we used the similar expression *multiplies<int>()* in the following call to specify that multiplication is required:

```
int prod = accumulate(a, a+N, 1, multiplies<int>());
```

Here is the complete list of such templates (defined in the header *functional*) as far as they correspond to the well-known standard binary operators:

```
plus<T>              minus<T>
multiplies<T>        divides<T>         modulus<T>
equal_to<T>          not_equal_to<T>
greater<T>           less<T>
greater_equal<T>     less_equal<T>
logical_and<T>       logical_or<T>
```

As we know, expressions such as *plus<T>*( ) are objects; in other words, the above templates, followed by parentheses, are standard function objects, provided by STL. There are also some templates corresponding with the unary operators – (as used in –*x*) and ! (pronounced *not*):

```
negate<T>            logical_not<T>
```

We now return to the program *countvw2.cpp* at the end of the last section. This contains the call

```
int n = count_if(p, p + strlen(p), found);
```

where *found* was a function of our own, indicating which characters are to be counted. Now suppose that we want to count all characters *ch* >= '*k*'. Obviously, it would then be possible to replace the *found* function with the following one:

```
bool found(char ch)
{   return ch >= 'k';
}
```

Instead, we can use the above template *greater_equal<T>* but then some means is necessary to bind *greater_equal<char>* to the value '*k*'. We do this by writing

```
bind2nd(greater_equal<char>(), 'k')
```

This expression can replace the function name *found* in the above call to *count_if*, giving

```
n = count_if(p, p + strlen(p),
   bind2nd(greater_equal<char>(), 'k'));
```

The template *bind2nd* is called a *binder*, which is a special case of a *function adaptor*. Since the two expressions

```
ch >= 'k'      and        !(ch < 'k')
```

are equivalent, we may wonder if we can use some form equivalent to the latter expression as the third argument of *count_if*. This is indeed possible, provided we use another kind of function adaptor, called a *negator*:

```
n = count_if(p, p + strlen(p),
    not1(bind2nd(less<char>(), 'k')));
```

We will discuss function (and other) adaptors in greater detail in Chapter 6.

2.5 Introduction to Associative Containers

Besides arrays and lists, used for the sequence containers (array, vector, deque and list) discussed so far, *balanced trees* form another classical data structure to store and retrieve data efficiently. They form the basis for another group of containers provided by STL, called (*sorted*) *associative containers*. As we have done before, we will focus on *using* these containers rather than on their implementation. There are four types: sets, multisets, maps and multimaps. Before discussing their use, let us first see how they differ.

Sets

Each element of a *set* is identical with its key, and keys are unique. Because of this, two distinct elements of a set cannot be equal. For example, a set can consist of the following elements:

```
123

124
800
950
```

Multisets

A *multiset* differs from a set only in that it can contain equal elements. For example we can have a multiset consisting of the following four elements:

```
123
123
800
950
```

Maps

Each element of a *map* has several members, one of which is the key. No two keys of a map can be equal. For example, a map can consist of the following four elements, each having a numerical key and alphabetic satellite data:

```
123    John
124    Mary
800    Alexander
950    Jim
```

Multimaps

A *multimap* differs from a map in that duplicated keys are allowed. For example, here is a multimap consisting of four elements (with numerical key):

```
123    John
123    Mary
800    Alexander
950    Jim
```

In contrast to sequence containers, associative containers keep their elements sorted, regardless of the way these are inserted.

Headers and portability

In the original HP version of STL, there were four headers associated with the subjects under consideration: *set.h*, *multiset.h*, *map.h* and *multimap.h*. In the Draft C++ Standard, there are only two: *set* and *map*. These are to be used also for multisets and multimaps.

2.6 Sets and Multisets

In this section and the next, we will discuss a single, simple program for each of the four associative container types; these two sections are not complete with regard to all possible operations for these containers, but they should make their most important characteristics very clear.

Sets

Let us begin with two sets of integers. Although elements are inserted in different ways, the resulting sets are identical:

```cpp
// set2.cpp: Two identical sets, created differently.
#include <iostream>
#include <set>
using namespace std;

int main()
{   set<int, less<int> > S, T;
    S.insert(10); S.insert(20); S.insert(30);
    S.insert(10);
    T.insert(20); T.insert(30); T.insert(10);
    if (S == T) cout << "Equal sets, containing:\n";
    for (set<int, less<int> >::iterator i = T.begin();
        i != T.end(); i++)
            cout << *i << " ";
    cout << endl;
    return 0;
}
```

This program gives the output

```
Equal sets, containing:
10 20 30
```

which demonstrates that the order 20, 30, 10, in which the elements of T were inserted is irrelevant; neither does set S change when the element 10 for the second time. Remember, keys are unique in sets but can be duplicated in multisets as we will see in a moment.

Notice the peculiar way the sets S and T are defined:

```
set<int, less<int> > S, T;
```

The predicate

```
less<int>
```

is required to specify the meaning of $k_1 < k_2$ where k_1 and k_2 are keys. This looks very strange in the present example, where these keys are integers, but remember, the set container can also be used with keys of user-defined types (instead of *int*). The blank space in

```
less<int> >
```

prevents confusion with the operator >>.

Although sets are not sequences, we can apply both iterators and the functions *begin* and *end* to them, as this program illustrates. These iterators are bidirectional (see Section 1.9): with iterator i of type *set<int, less<int> >::iterator*, the expressions $++i$, $i++$, $--i$, and $i--$ are valid, but $i + N$ and $i - N$ are not.

Multisets

The following program shows that equal keys can occur in multisets. Just for a change, let us use the *copy* function for output, as discussed in Section 1.9:

```
// multiset.cpp: Two multisets.
#include <iostream>
#include <set>
using namespace std;

int main()
{   multiset<int, less<int> > S, T;
    S.insert(10); S.insert(20); S.insert(30);
    S.insert(10);
    T.insert(20); T.insert(30); T.insert(10);
    if (S == T) cout << "Equal multisets:\n"; else
                cout << "Unequal multisets:\n";
```

```
cout << "S: ";
   copy(S.begin(), S.end(),
      ostream_iterator<int>(cout, " "));
   cout << endl;
   cout << "T: ";
   copy(T.begin(), T.end(),
      ostream_iterator<int>(cout, " "));
   cout << endl;
   return 0;
}
```

The output of this program shows that the key 10 occurs twice in the multiset S. Since it occurs only once in T, these two multisets are unequal:

```
Unequal multisets:
S: 10 10 20 30
T: 10 20 30
```

2.7 Maps and Multimaps

Maps

The term associative container becomes clear when we are dealing with maps. For example, a telephone directory associates names with numbers. With a given name, also known as a *key*, we want the corresponding number. In other words, a phone book is a mapping from names to numbers. If the name *Johnson, J.* corresponds with number 12345, STL enables us to establish a map D so that we can write the following statement to express the mapping shown on the second line:

```
D["Johnson, J."] = 12345;
```

"Johnson, J." $\rightarrow$ 12345

Note that this is similar to conventional arrays, such as

```
a[5] = 'Q';
```

5                $\rightarrow$ *'Q'*

In the latter case, subscript values are 0, 1, 2, ..., while this restriction no longer applies to maps. The following program shows that maps are easy to use:

```
// map1.cpp: First application of a map.
#include <iostream>
#include <string>
#include <map>
using namespace std;
```

```
class compare {
public:
   bool operator()(const char *s, const char *t)const
   {  return strcmp(s, t) < 0;
   }
};

int main()
{  map<char*, long, compare> D;
   D["Johnson, J."]  = 12345;
   D["Smith, P."]    = 54321;
   D["Shaw, A."]     = 99999;
   D["Atherton, K."] = 11111;
   char GivenName[30];
   cout << "Enter a name: ";
   cin.get(GivenName, 30);
   if (D.find(GivenName) != D.end())
      cout << "The number is " << D[GivenName];
   else
      cout << "Not found.";
   cout << endl;
   return 0;
}
```

In contrast to our previous example, program *map.cpp* contains a function object of our own, as discussed in Section 1.12. The definition

```
map<char*, long, compare> D;
```

of the directory D contains three template arguments:

- type *char** of the key;
- type *long* of the satellite data;
- the function object class *compare*.

The *operator*() member function of *compare* specifies the *less than* relation for keys.

Multimaps

The following program shows that multimaps can contain equal keys:

```
// multimap.cpp: A multimap containing equal keys.
#include <iostream>
#include <string>
#include <map>

using namespace std;
```

```
class compare {
public:
    bool operator()(const char *s, const char *t)const
    {   return strcmp(s, t) < 0;
    }
};

typedef multimap<char*, long, compare> mmtype;

int main()
{   mmtype D;
    D.insert(mmtype::value_type("Johnson, J.", 12345));
    D.insert(mmtype::value_type("Smith, P.", 54321));
    D.insert(mmtype::value_type("Johnson, J.", 10000));
    cout << "There are " << D.size() << " elements.\n";
    return 0;
}
```

Its output is:

```
There are 3 elements.
```

The subscripting operator is not defined for multimaps, so we cannot insert an element by writing, for example,

```
D["Johnson, J."]  = 12345;
```

Instead, we write

```
D.insert(mmtype::value_type("Johnson, J.", 12345));
```

where *mmtype* actually means

```
multimap<char*, long, compare>
```

Since the identifier *value_type* is defined inside the *multimap* template class, the prefix *mmtype*:: preceding *value_type* is required here. The definition of this identifier *value_type* is based on the template *pair*, which we will discuss now.

2.8 Pairs and Comparisons

To do more interesting things with maps and multimaps, we need to be familiar with the *pair* template class, which is also useful for other purposes. It is defined in the header *utility*. The following program uses this class:

```
// pairs.cpp: Operations on pairs.

#include <iostream>
#include <utility>

using namespace std;

int main()
{  pair<int, double> P(123, 4.5), Q = P;
   Q = make_pair(122, 4.5);
   cout << "P: " << P.first << " " << P.second << endl;
   cout << "Q: " << Q.first << " " << Q.second << endl;
   if (P > Q) cout << "P > Q\n";
   ++Q.first;
   cout << "After ++Q.first: ";
   if (P == Q) cout << "P == Q\n";
   return 0;
}
```

Most programs that use STL will contain a #*include* line for some header that invokes *utility* indirectly. For example, if there is a line #*include <vector>* in our program, we can omit the line #*include <utility>*.

As this program illustrates, the *pair* template takes two template arguments, the types of the *pair* data members *first* and *second*. The *pair* constructor, used for *P*, takes two initial values for these data members. There is no default constructor for a *pair*; in other words, we cannot write

```
pair<int, double> P;    // error
```

Instead of supplying the two pair elements explicitly, as done in the program for *P*, we can supply an already existing pair, as the above definition for *Q* demonstrates. Incidentally, we may replace = *P* with (*P*) in this definition of *Q*.

After defining *Q*, we could have assigned a different value to it by writing

```
Q = pair<int, double>(122, 4.5);
```

Instead, we have used the shorter statement:

```
Q = make_pair(122, 4.5);
```

which has the same effect. For any two pairs *P* and *Q*, the values of the expressions *P* == *Q* and *P* < *Q*, and so on, are in accordance with the well-known lexicographical ordering, as these examples illustrate:

```
(122, 5.5) <  (123, 4.5)
(123, 4.5) <  (123, 5.5)
(123, 4.5) == (123, 4.5)
```

In program *pairs.cpp*, we initially have $P > Q$, but after increasing *Q.first* by one, P and Q become equal, as the following output of this program demonstrates:

```
P: 123 4.5
Q: 122 4.5
P > Q
After ++Q.first: P == Q
```

Comparisons

When writing comparison operators for our own types, we have to define only == and <. The four remaining operators, !=, >, <= and >= are then automatically defined by the STL by these four templates:

```
template <class T1, class T2>
inline bool operator!=(const T1 &x, const T2 &y)
{   return !(x == y);
}

template <class T1, class T2>
inline bool operator>(const T1 &x, const T2 &y)
{   return y < x;
}

template <class T1, class T2>
inline bool operator<=(const T1 &x, const T2 &y)
{   return !(y < x);
}

template <class T1, class T2>
inline bool operator>=(const T1 &x, const T2 &y)
{   return !(x < y);
}
```

As you can see, these four very general templates define !=, >, <= and >= in terms of == and <. We need not write these four templates ourselves, because they occur in the header *functional*, which we implicitly use whenever we are using STL.

2.9 Maps Revisited

Since a map contains pairs (k, d), where k is a key and d satellite data, we can expect the *pair* template to be useful for maps. In the same way as for a sequence container, we can use an iterator i for an associative container; then the expression *i denotes a pair, (*i).first* being the key and (*i).second* the satellite data. For example, using iterator i and the same map as in Section 2.7, we can display the entire map contents (with the keys in ascending order) by using the following for-loop:

```
for (i = D.begin(); i != D.end(); i++)
   cout << setw(9)
        << (*i).second << " "
        << (*i).first << endl;
```

Note that in this way we display the *(*i).second* before *(*i).first*, so that we need not worry about how many positions to reserve for the names in output such as

```
54321 Papadimitriou, C.
12345 Smith, J.
```

This format is also easier to deal with in input operations, because in this way we can read, in this order, a number, one blank space and a string ending at the end of the line. But remember, this string is the key, despite its position at the end of the line.

The above for-loop actually occurs in the program we will now discuss. This is again about a telephone directory, but this time we can perform quite a few operations. To keep the program reasonably simple, the commands are not very user-friendly, as the following table, based on examples, shows:

Example of a command	*Meaning*
?Johnson, J.	Display telephone number of *Johnson, J.*
/Johnson, J.	Delete *Johnson, J.* from phonebook
!66331 Peterson, K.	Insert *Peterson, K.* with phone number 66331
*	List the entire phonebook
=	Save phonebook to file *phone.txt*
#	Exit

When we start program *map2.cpp*, it tries to read data from the file *phone.txt*; if it exists, it should contain lines of text consisting of a phone number, one blank space and a name, in that order. Names may contain blank spaces, as the above table illustrates. The user must enter the names exactly in the form they are given, including such blank spaces.

Program *map2.cpp* is based on string-handling in the spirit of C. The keys are not really the names themselves but rather pointers to character sequences stored elsewhere. This approach may appeal to experienced C programmers, but it is not very elegant and we must be very careful not to make memory allocation and deallocation errors. In Section 2.12, we will discuss a simpler, but possibly less portable version of this program, based on the *string* library class.

```cpp
// map2.cpp: Second application of a map:
//           a telephone directory.
#include <iostream>
#include <fstream>
#include <iomanip>
#include <stdlib.h>
#include <string>
#include <map>
using namespace std;
const int maxlen = 200;

class compare {
public:
   bool operator()(const char *s, const char *t)const
   { return strcmp(s, t) < 0;
   }
};

typedef map<char*, long, compare> directype;

void ReadInput(directype &D)
{  ifstream ifstr("phone.txt");
   long nr;
   char buf[maxlen], *p;
   if (ifstr)
   {  cout << "Entries read from file phone.txt:\n";
      for (;;)
      {  ifstr >> nr;
         ifstr.get(); // skip space
         ifstr.getline(buf, maxlen);
         if (!ifstr) break;
         cout << setw(9) << nr << " " << buf << endl;
         p = new char[strlen(buf) + 1];
         strcpy(p, buf);
         D[p] = nr;
      }
   }
   ifstr.close();
}

void ShowCommands()
{  cout <<
      "Commands: ?name        : find phone number,\n"
      "          /name        : delete\n"
      "          !number name: insert (or update)\n"
      "          *            : list whole phonebook\n"
      "          =            : save in file\n"
      "          #            : exit" << endl;
}
```

```
void ProcessCommands(directype &D)
{  ofstream ofstr;
   long nr;
   char ch, buf[maxlen], *p;
   directype::iterator i;
   for (;;)
   {  cin >> ch; // skip any white-space and read ch.
      switch (ch){
      case '?': case '/': // find or delete:
         cin.getline(buf, maxlen);
         i = D.find(buf);
         if (i == D.end()) cout << "Not found.\n";
         else              // Key found
         if (ch == '?')    // 'Find' command
            cout << "Number: " << (*i).second << endl;
         else              // 'Delete' command
         {  delete[] (*i).first; D.erase(i);
         }
         break;
      case '!':              // insert (or update)
         cin >> nr;
         if (cin.fail())
         {  cout << "Usage: !number name\n";
            cin.clear(); cin.getline(buf, maxlen);
            break;
         }
         cin.get();          // skip space;
         cin.getline(buf, maxlen);
         i = D.find(buf);
         if (i == D.end())
         {  p = new char[strlen(buf) + 1];
            strcpy(p, buf);
            D[p] = nr;
         } else (*i).second = nr;
         break;
      case '*':
         for (i = D.begin(); i != D.end(); i++)
            cout << setw(9) << (*i).second << " "
                 << (*i).first << endl;
         break;
      case '=':
         ofstr.open("phone.txt");
         if (ofstr)
         {  for (i = D.begin(); i != D.end(); i++)
               ofstr << setw(9) << (*i).second << " "
                     << (*i).first << endl;
            ofstr.close();
         } else cout << "Cannot open output file.\n";
         break;
```

```
         case '#': break;
         default:
             cout << "Use: * (list), ? (find), = (save), "
                 "/ (delete), ! (insert), or # (exit).\n";
             cin.getline(buf, maxlen);
             break;
         }
         if (ch == '#') break;
     }
}

int main()
{   directype D;
    ReadInput(D);
    ShowCommands();
    ProcessCommands(D);
    for (directype::iterator i = D.begin(); i != D.end();
        ++i) delete[] (*i).first;
    return 0;
}
```

To execute this program, there need not be an input file *phone.txt*. In the following demonstration there is such a file, containing two entries, for *Smith, P.* and *Johnson, J.* The data entered by the user is underlined. Note that in the phone book listings, generated by the command *, the names appear in alphabetic order. Remember, the names are the keys, even though they appear after the numbers:

```
Entries read from file phone.txt:
    54321 Smith, P.
    12345 Johnson, J.
Commands: ?name       : find phone number,
          /name        : delete
          !number name: insert (or update)
          *            : list whole phonebook
          =            : save in file
          #            : exit
!19723 Shaw, A.
*
    12345 Johnson, J.
    19723 Shaw, A.
    54321 Smith, P.
/Johnson, J.
*
    19723 Shaw, A.
    54321 Smith, P.
?Shaw, A.
Number: 19723

=
#
```

The strings are stored in memory allocated

```
p = new char[strlen(buf) + 1];
```

which is done both for the names read from the input file and for those entered by the user. Deallocation by executing

```
delete[] (*i).first;
```

is also done on two occasions: when the user enters a delete command, and at the end of the program, by way of cleaning up. Such actions will not occur in the version to be discussed in Section 2.12.

Equality expressed in terms of less-than

There is another interesting aspect related to C-style pointers used as keys. If a map is searched for a given key, we would expect that this is done by means of the equality operator $==$. Now suppose that in our program we search the map for a name, say, "*John*" and there is a map element containing this key "*John*". As every C(++) programmer ought to know, such a search must not be done by means of the $==$ operator because that would cause two addresses to be compared instead of the strings themselves. Instead of $==$, the function *strcmp* should be used. For example, with

```
char *s = "John", *t = "John";
```

the expressions

```
s == t
strcmp(s, t) == 0
```

will have the values 0 (=*false*) and 1 = (*true*), respectively.

Fortunately, tests for equality of two alphabetic keys will be done correctly in our program because our class *compare* is also used for this purpose. If we had to compare the numbers a and b, we could express the $==$ operator in terms of $<$ by replacing

```
a == b
```

with

```
!(a < b || b < a)
```

In the same way, testing whether two keys s and t, both of type *char**, refer to identical strings is done in our program as follows:

```
!(compare()(s, t) || compare()(t, s))
```

According to the *operator*( ) function in our class *compare*, this is equivalent to

```
!(strcmp(s, t) < 0 || strcmp(t, s) < 0)
```

Although slower, this is in turn equivalent to

```
strcmp(s, t) == 0
```

2.10 Other *insert* Functions

Inserting new entries is done in the last section by using the subscript operator in the following assignment statement:

```
D[p] = nr;
```

Instead of this assignment statement, we could have written

```
D.insert(directype::value_type(p, nr));
```

which is based both on our own definition

```
typedef map<char*, long, compare> directype;
```

and on the following definition of *value_type* inside the *map* template in the header *map*:

```
typedef pair<const Key, T> value_type;
```

where *Key* is the key type and *T* the satellite-data type. The above rather complicated call to the *insert* function has no advantages over the much simpler assignment statement if we ignore the value returned by *insert*. This value can provide us with useful information about the insertion process. Let us have a look at the way this *insert* function is declared in the header *map*:

```
pair<iterator, bool> insert(const value_type &x);
```

Apparently, *insert* returns a *pair* object, consisting of both an iterator, denoting the position of the inserted (or replaced) entry and a *bool* value indicating whether a new entry has been inserted. This can be useful in other applications. In program *map2.cpp* it is not, because when the user enters a name we begin by investigating whether this name is new. If it is not, we only change the associated phone number by executing

```
(*i).second = nr;
```

without performing any memory allocation or deallocation. Remember, the keys representing the names are actually C-style pointers.

We will also discuss another *insert* function for maps. If we know the position where the new element belongs, we can use this information to make insertion more efficient. In this case we had better use the *insert* function declared as

```
iterator insert(iterator position, const value_type &x);
```

This function returns the iterator value referring to the element that has just been inserted; we can use this value for the next insertion if a larger key follows. For example, if we know that all elements will be inserted in increasing order of their keys we can use an iterator *i* as is done in the following program:

```
// mapins.cpp: Fast insertion in a map.
#include <iostream>
#include <map>
using namespace std;

typedef map<int, double, less<int> > maptype;

int main()
{   maptype S;
    maptype::iterator i = S.end();
    for (int k=1; k<=10; k++)
       i = S.insert(i, maptype::value_type(k, 1.0/k));
    i = S.find(4);
    cout << (*i).second << endl; // Output: 0.25
    return 0;
}
```

The first argument of this insert version is used as a hint, indicating where to start searching. Inserting is fastest if the new element immediately follows the one referred to by the first argument. Insertion then takes constant time. By contrast, if the first argument refers to any other element already stored, insertion is also done correctly, but this will take $O(\log N)$ time, where N is the number of elements in the set.

2.11 Erasing Elements of a Map

To delete map elements, there are three *erase* member functions, declared as follows:

```
void erase(iterator position);
void erase(iterator first, iterator last);
size_type erase(const key_type &x);
```

We have used the first of these three in Section 2.9. The second enables us to erase all elements in a given range. The third is very easy to use because it only requires a key, not an iterator value. It returns 0 or 1, which is the number of elements that are erased. In other words, if there is an element with the given key, the function returns 1; if there is not, it returns 0.

2.12 More Convenient Strings

So far, our way of manipulating strings has been rather primitive. For example, in program *map.cpp* of Section 2.9, we had to perform the two statements

```
delete[] (*i).first;
D.erase(i);
```

to erase the set element referred to by iterator *i*. Omitting the first of these would have caused 'memory leakage', since the actual string of characters would then remain somewhere in memory (starting at the address stored in (*i).*first*) without any possibility for us to use it after the second of these two statements is executed. Our way of string handling has been in the spirit of C, not of C++. The keys of our map elements were pointers to memory locations that we allocated and deallocated ourselves.

The Draft C++ Standard provides a library string class, to make string manipulation easier and less error-prone. This *string* class does not belong to STL and it is not yet supported by all C++ compilers. In other words, programs based on this class are currently not portable. Hopefully, this will change in the future. Here we will discuss some aspects of this class, which is supported by BC5 and VC5.

To define *string* variables, we have to use the following #include line:

```
#include <string>
```

and this time we must not write *<string.h>* instead of *<string>*. If your compiler does not accept this, there may be a header *bstring.h* or *cstring.h* which you can use instead. It may be necessary to place this #include line for string handling *before* those for STL. Then we can write, for example, the following assignments:

```
string s, t;
s = "ABC";
t = "DEFGH";
s = t;          // s = "DEFGH"
s = 'A';        // s = "A"
```

As this fragment shows, the right-hand side in such assignments can be any of three types:

- *string* (in *s* = *t*;)
- *char** (in *s* = "ABC";)
- *char* (in *s* = 'A';).

The same applies to the operator +=, used to append the second operand to the first, which is of type *string*:

```
string s, t("KLM"), u(t);
                 // s = "", t = u = "KLM"
s += t;          // s = "KLM"
s += "PQR";      // s = "KLMPQR"
s += 'W';        // s = "KLMPQRW"
```

This fragment also shows that we can initialize a string, using a value either of type *char** or of type *string*.

There are two other interesting ways of initializing strings. First we can supply a repetition factor; for example the initial value of *s* will be "AAAAA" if we write

```
string s(5, 'A');
```

Second, we can use a pair of iterators, as in

```
string t(v.begin(), v.end()),
       u(a, a+3);
```

where *v* can have type *vector<char>*, and *a* is a *char* array the first three elements of which are used to initialize *u*.

Class *string* has a member function, *c_str*( ), returning a pointer of type *const char**, which we can use for traditional C-style string operations. For example, after

```
string s("AB");
char a[10];
strcpy(a, s.c_str());
```

we have

```
a[0] = 'A'
a[1] = 'B'
a[2] = '\0'
```

As with a vector, we obtain the current size of a string by using the *size* member function. For example, after defining *s* as is done in the above fragment, we have

```
s.size() = 2
```

There are many more interesting string facilities, some of which are demonstrated by the following program:

```
// strdemo.cpp: String demonstration program.

#include <iostream>
#include <string>

using namespace std;

int main()
{  string s(5, 'A'), t("BC"), u;
   u = s + t;
   cout << "u = s + t = " << u << endl;
   cout << "u.size() = " << u.size() << endl;
   cout << "u[6] = " << u[6] << endl;
   cout << "Enter two new strings s and t:\n";
   cin >> s >> t;
   cout << "s.size() = " << s.size() << endl;
   cout << (s < t ? "s < t" : "s >= t");
   cout << endl;
   return 0;
}
```

As this program illustrates, we can use the operator + (in addition to +=, discussed above) to concatenate two strings. The operators << and >> are available for output and input and they behave in the same way as with conventional strings. This also applies to the subscripting operator, as demonstrated here by displaying the value of $u[6]$. Finally, we can use the operators ==, !=, <, >, <= and >= to compare strings, as demonstrated here for the operator <. Here is a demonstration of this program, in which text entered by the user is underlined:

```
u = s + t = AAAAABC
u.size() = 7
u[6] = C
Enter two new strings s and t:
xxxxx xxy
s.size() = 5
s < t
```

Despite their differences in length, strings can be elements of arrays and of STL containers, as the following program shows:

```
// strelem.cpp: Strings as elements of list L and
//    array a.
#include <iostream>
#include <string>
#include <list>
#include <algorithm>
using namespace std;
```

```
int main()
{  string s("One"), t("Two"), u("Three");
   list<string> L;
   L.push_back(s);
   L.push_back(t);
   L.push_back(u);
   string a[3];
   copy(L.begin(), L.end(), a);
   for (int k=0; k<3; k++) cout << a[k] << endl;
   return 0;
}
```

As you will expect, this program produces the following output:

```
One
Two
Three
```

Let us now use the class *string* for a second solution to the problem discussed in Section 2.9. Recall that program *map2.cpp* tried to read a file *phone.txt*, to be used as a telephone directory. If there is no such file, we can use the program to create one. Program *map2a.cpp* is different in that it does not apply the *new* and *delete* operators for C-style strings, but uses the new string type instead. Some comments of the form '// !' indicate points where this program differs from *map2.cpp*:

```
// map2a.cpp: Second version of telephone directory,
//                based on type 'string'.
#include <iostream>
#include <fstream>
#include <iomanip>
#include <string>
#include <map>
using namespace std;
                                                         // !
typedef map<string, long, less<string> > directype;

// Read all characters until '\n' and store them in str,
// except for '\n', which is read but not stored.
void getaline(istream &is, string &str)
{  char ch;
   str = "";                                             // !
   for (;;)
   {  is.get(ch);
      if (is.fail() || ch == '\n') break;
      str += ch;
   }
}
```

```
void ReadInput(directype &D)
{  ifstream ifstr("phone.txt");
   long nr;
   string str;                                        // !
   if (ifstr)
   {  cout << "Entries read from file phone.txt:\n";
      for (;;)
      {  ifstr >> nr;
         ifstr.get(); // skip space
         getaline(ifstr, str);                        // !
         if (!ifstr) break;
         cout << setw(9) << nr << " " << str << endl;
         D[str] = nr;                                 // !
      }
   }
   ifstr.close();
}

void ShowCommands()
{  cout <<
      "Commands: ?name      : find phone number,\n"
      "          /name      : delete\n"
      "          !number name: insert (or update)\n"
      "          *          : list whole phonebook\n"
      "          =          : save in file\n"
      "          #          : exit" << endl;
}

void ProcessCommands(directype &D)
{  ofstream ofstr;
   long nr;
   string str;                                        // !
   char ch;
   directype::iterator i;
   for (;;)
   {  cin >> ch; // skip any white-space and read ch.
      switch (ch){
      case '?': case '/': // find or delete:
         getaline(cin, str);
         i = D.find(str);                             // !
         if (i == D.end())
            cout << "Not found.\n";
         else            // Key found
         if (ch == '?')  // 'Find' command
            cout << "Number: " << (*i).second << endl;
         else            // 'Delete' command
            D.erase(i);                               // !
         break;
```

```cpp
      case '!':                      // insert (or update)
         cin >> nr;
         if (cin.fail())
         {  cout << "Usage: !number name\n";
            cin.clear();
            getaline(cin, str);                              // !
            break;
         }
         cin.get();              // skip space;
         getaline(cin, str);
         D[str] = nr;                                        // !
         break;
      case '*':
         for (i = D.begin(); i != D.end(); i++)
            cout << setw(9) << (*i).second << " "
                 << (*i).first << endl;
         break;
      case '=':
         ofstr.open("phone.txt");
         if (ofstr)
         {  for (i = D.begin(); i != D.end(); i++)
               ofstr << setw(9) << (*i).second << " "
                     << (*i).first << endl;
            ofstr.close();
         } else cout << "Cannot open output file.\n";
         break;
      case '#': break;
      default:
         cout << "Use: * (list), ? (find), = (save), "
              "/ (delete), ! (insert), or # (exit).\n";
         getaline(cin, str); break;                          // !
      }
      if (ch == '#') break;
   }
}


int main()
{  directype D;
   ReadInput(D);
   ShowCommands();
   ProcessCommands(D);
   return 0;                                                // !
}
```

Since this program behaves in the same way as its original version, *map2.cpp*, we will omit another demonstration. This version is easier in that we manipulate *string* objects in the same way as built-in types, such as *int*, despite any differences in string lengths. Since memory for these strings is allocated and deallocated automatically, the operators *new* and *delete* do not occur in the program.

3

Sequence Containers

3.1 Vectors and Related Types

When dealing with templates in general and STL in particular, the beginner is often confused by the rather complicated syntax. We will therefore begin with a brief discussion of this, using examples that are not necessary practical but nevertheless useful because they clarify this syntax.

In Chapter 2 we have been using the type *value_type* when dealing with associative containers. This type is also available for sequence containers. It is defined in the *vector* class in the following, rather trivial way

```
typedef T value_type;
```

while it is defined in the *map* class as

```
typedef pair<const Key, T> value_type;
```

In either case, we can see that *value_type* denotes the type of the elements stored in the container. Since its definition is inside the class in question, we have to qualify the name *value_type* when we are using it outside the class, writing, for example,

```
vector<int>::value_type
```

It follows from the above discussion that this complicated form simply means *int*. In other words, if we are using the header *vector* we can replace the line

```
int k;
```

with

```
vector<int>::value_type k;
```

This is hardly an improvement, but it shows that there is nothing mysterious about the form *vector<int>::value_type*.

The types listed below are similar to this form in that we can use them like types denoted by single identifiers:

```
vector<int>::iterator
vector<int>::reverse_iterator
vector<int>::const_iterator
vector<int>::const_reverse_iterator
```

Recall that we have introduced the first three of these four types in Sections 1.2 and 1.3. It will be clear that the fourth is to be used if we traverse the container backward while not changing the elements. It is often convenient to simplify the notation of types by means of typedef declarations. For example, after

```
typedef vector<int>::iterator VecIntIterType;
```

we can replace

```
vector<int>::iterator i;
```

with the simpler line

```
VecIntIterType i;
```

Here is complete summary of locally defined types:

```
value_type
reference, const_reference
iterator, const_iterator,
reverse_iterator, const_reverse_iterator
difference_type
size_type
vector_allocator
```

Their names indicate very well what they are about. We will use most of them in our discussions of container member functions. For example, as we will see shortly, there are two subscripting operators for vectors, which can be declared inside the *vector* template as follows:

```
reference operator[](size_type n);
```

```
const_reference operator[](size_type n) const;
```

If we are dealing with type *vector<int>*, type *reference* stands for *int&*, or *reference-to-int*. Type *difference_type* is a signed integral type that can represent the difference between two iterators, while *size_type* is the same as *difference_type* but unsigned instead of signed.

Type *vector<bool>*

Vectors of *bool* elements are handled as a special case, so that they can be efficiently packed: it would be a waste of memory if each element, requiring only one bit, occupied a whole word. Obviously, a special treatment of type *vector<bool>* is possible only if *bool* is a built-in type, not just another way of writing the word *int*. Recall that we have discussed this subject in Section 1.1.

The member function *flip( )* is available for type *vector<bool>*, not for type *vector<int>*. It inverts either all bits or only one selected bit of a vector, as the following examples show:

```
vector<bool> b(100); // 100 bits, all reset to 0
b.flip(); // All bits inverted so they are now 1
b[73].flip();
cout << b[72] << b[73] << b[74]; // Output: 101
```

There is also the member function *swap* to exchange two Boolean vectors. For example, after

```
vector<bool> u(100, true), v(50, false);
u.swap(v);
cout << u.size() << " "
     << v.size() << " "
     << u[0];                        // Output:  50 100 0
```

The following program uses a Boolean vector to implement the sieve of Erastos‐thenes. This is a well-known, efficient method to generate prime numbers 2, 3, 5, 7, 11, 13, ... The elements of a Boolean vector S, the *sieve*, are initially set to *true*, and some are later set to false:

$S[i] = true$ means: i may be a prime number (no divisor found yet);
$S[i] = false$ means: i is not a prime number (because it is a multiple of some smaller prime number).

To limit the amount of output, the following program does not display a long list of prime numbers. Instead, it counts how many prime numbers there are below a given value N and it also displays the largest of them:

```cpp
// erastos.cpp: Sieve of Erastosthenes to generate
//     all prime numbers below a given limit.

#include <iostream>
#include <vector>
#include <math.h>

using namespace std;

int main()
{   cout <<
        "To generate all prime numbers < N, enter N: ";
    long N, i, sqrtN, count = 0, j;
    cin >> N;
    sqrtN = int(sqrt(N)) + 1;
    vector<bool> S(N, true);

    // Initially, all S[i] are true.
    // S[i] = false if and when
    // we find i is not a prime number.
    // some prime number.

    for (i=2; i < sqrtN; i++)
        if (S[i])
            for (int k=i*i; k<N; k+=i) S[k] = false;

    for (i=2; i<N; i++)
        if (S[i]) {j = i; count++;}

    cout << "There are " << count
         << " prime numbers less than N.\n";
    cout << "Largest prime number less than N is "
         << j << "." << endl;
    return 0;
}
```

The following demonstration shows that the number of prime numbers generated can really be too large to display them all on the screen:

```
To generate all prime numbers < N, enter N: 1000000
There are 78498 prime numbers less than N.
Largest prime number less than N is 999983.
```

The computing time required for this demonstration was about 10s on a 486 computer, which demonstrates that the 'sieve of Erastosthenes' provides a very fast way of generating prime numbers. Besides, it shows that Boolean vectors are not only convenient but also efficient.

3.2 The *capacity* and *reserve* Functions

So far we have taken it for granted that vectors are of flexible size, not worrying about how they are implemented. Now suppose we want to add an element to a vector, so that the size of that vector will increase by 1. If this happens a great many times, it would be very inefficient to reallocate memory each time, since this may require copying all elements to a memory area that can accommodate the enlarged vector. It is much better to allocate more memory space than is actually required, so that, in most cases, additional memory is already available when the vector needs to grow. The number of elements of vector v for which memory is allocated is equal to

```
v.capacity()
```

This value is greater than or equal to $v.size()$, as Figure 3.1 illustrates.

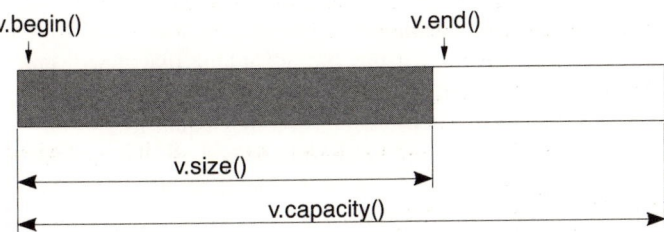

Figure 3.1 *Size and capacity of a vector v*

The following program shows that $v.capacity()$ remains constant for a long time when vector v gradually grows, while $v.size()$ increases by one each time a new element is added to v:

```
// capacity.cpp: The capacity member function
//               for vectors.

#include <iostream>
#include <iomanip>
#include <vector>

using namespace std;

int main()
{  vector<int> v;
   vector<int>::size_type n0 = 12345, n1;
   cout << "v.size()  v.capacity()\n";
```

```
        for (long i=0L; i<100000L; i++)
        {   n1 = v.capacity();
            if (n1 != n0)
            {   cout << setw(8) << v.size() << "        "
                    << setw(8) << n1 << endl;
                n0 = n1;
            }
            v.push_back(123); // v.size() increases by 1
        }
        return 0;
}
```

In this program the size of vector *v* grows from 0 to 99 999. The number of vector elements for which memory is reallocated, *v.capacity*(), is displayed each time this differs from what it was in the previous step. The values stored in the vector being irrelevant to our present purpose, all vector elements are made equal to 123 here. Initially, the vector is empty and both *v.size*() and *v.capacity*() are zero. After insertion of the very first element, *v.size*() is 1, but *v.capacity*(), the number of elements for which memory is allocated, is equal to some rather large value. With BC5, this value is 256, with some other STL versions it is 1024. Although this may seem to be a waste of memory, it has the advantage that it will take a long time before reallocation is required, since this capacity of, say, 256 is used for all vector sizes 1, 2, 3, ..., 256. Only when *v.size*() becomes equal to 257 do we need to re-allocate memory. In the STL implementation used here, the capacity is then made twice as large, so that enough memory is available for the sizes 257, 258, ... 512. This principle of doubling memory space as soon as reallocation is required is consistently applied, as (with BC5) the following output of the program shows:

```
v.size()   v.capacity()
       0              0
       1            256
     257            512
     513           1024
    1025           2048
    2049           4096
    4097           8192
    8193          16384
   16385          32768
   32769          65536
   65537         131072
```

The function *capacity* gives information memory allocation; there is a related function, *reserve*, which gives us control over it. After the execution of the call

```
v.reserve(n);
```

the value of *v.capacity*( ) is at least *n*. The function *reserve* may speed up program execution if we know in advance how many elements vector *v* will eventually have. For example, in program *capacity.cpp*, if we insert the line

```
v.reserve(100000);
```

just before the for-statement, this program will produce only the following two output lines:

```
v.size()  v.capacity()
       0        100000
```

Memory allocation now occurs only once. After the above call to *reserve*, there is enough room in the vector for all 100000 elements that are inserted in the for-statement.

Reallocation, iterator values and *reserve*

When, due to its growth, reallocation of vector *v* takes place, resulting in an increased value of *v.capacity*( ), any iterator values referring to elements of *v* will in general become invalid. This will be clear if we think of iterators as pointers, containing addresses. Reallocation may require the whole vector to be moved to other memory locations and we cannot expect any automatic updates of iterators that in the past have been used for these vectors. For example,

```
vector<int> v, w;
...
vector<int>::iterator i;
v.push_back(0);
i = v.begin();
for (long k=1L; k<100000L; k++)
   v.push_back(k);
cout << (*i);  // ???
```

In the last line of this fragment, *i* refers to a memory location that may not belong to vector *v* any more. This is similar to visiting an old acquaintance at the address at which he or she used to live but which is now inhabited by other people. However, there is an exception; if the second line (indicated by three dots) of the above fragment consists of the statement

```
v.reserve(N);
```

where $N \geq 100\,000$, then no reallocation takes place in the for-loop, so that *i* remains equal to *v.begin*( ).

As we have seen in Section 1.9, we can use the expressions $i + n$ and $i - n$, where *i* is an iterator and *n* an integer, for vectors (as we can for deques, but not for lists). This provides a safe way of storing the positions of vectors:

```
vector<int> v;
vector<int>::iterator i;
int k;
for (...) v.push_back(...);
i = ...;
k = i - v.begin();          // *i == v[k]
for (...) v.push_back(...);
// Extending v may cause reallocation, which would
// make *i undefined.
i = v.begin() + k;          // *i == v[k] again.
// Iterator i now refers to the same element as it did
// originally, although this element may be moved to
// a different location.
```

As indicated in the above comment, we do not really need iterators to access vector elements: the convenient subscripting operator [] for arrays is also available for vectors, so at the end of the above fragment we can write $v[k]$ instead of $*i$. In general, we can write

```
v[k]          instead of          *(v.begin() + k)
```

The (rather inefficient) vector member function *erase*, introduced in Section 1.3, also invalidates all iterators referring to vector elements following the one that is erased, since these elements will be moved to fill the gap caused by the erase operation.

3.3 Summary of *vector* Member Functions

All vector member functions are listed below, along with a reference or a brief description. Their declarations below could occur in the header *vector*, although many member functions are actually completely *defined* rather than only *declared* in this header:

```
iterator begin();
iterator end();
void push_back(const T& x);
reverse_iterator rbegin();
reverse_iterator rend();
```
   Discussed in Section 1.2.

```
const_iterator begin() const;
const_iterator end() const;
```
   As discussed in Section 1.3 for lists.

```
const_reverse_iterator rbegin() const;
const_reverse_iterator rend() const;
```
For reverse traversal, in read-only mode.

```
size_type size() const;
size_type capacity() const;
void reserve(size_type n);
```
Discussed in Section 3.2.

```
size_type max_size() const;
```
A very large integer (such as $1\,073\,741\,823$) indicating how large the vector can grow.

```
bool empty() const;
```
Indicates whether the vector is empty.

```
vector();                                          // (1)
vector(size_type n, const T& value = T());         // (2)
vector(const vector<T>& x);                        // (3)
vector(const_iterator first, const_iterator last); // (4)
~vector();
```
Four constructors and a destructor. These four constructors are used in these examples:

```
    vector<int> v;          // (1) Default constructor.
    vector<int> w(5, -3);   // (2) Generates five elements,
                            //       all equal to -3.
    vector<int> w(5);       // (2) Generates five elements.
    vector<int> w1(w);      // (3) Copy constructor.
    vector<int> w2(w.begin()+11, w.begin()+15);
                            // (4) Copies five elements
                            //       from w to w2.
```

```
reference operator[](size_type n);
const_reference operator[](size_type n) const;
```
Subscripting operators, both used in

```
    w[3] = 3 * w[2] + 1;
```

```
vector<T>& operator=(const vector<T>& x);
```
Assignment operator, as used in

```
    vector<int> w(5, -3), v;
    v = w;
```

```
reference front();
reference back();
const_reference front() const;
const_reference back() const;
```

These functions give access to the first and to the final elements of a vector. For example, we can write

```
vector<int> v;
for (int i=10; i<15; i++) v.push_back(i);
v.front() = 1000;
cout << v.front() << " " << v.back() << "    ";
cout << "Size = " << v.size() << endl;
// Output: 1000 14    Size = 5
```

```
void swap(vector<T>& x);
```
We can write either

```
v.swap(w);
```
or

```
w.swap(v);
```

to exchange the vectors *v* and *w* of the same type (but not necessarily of the same size).

```
iterator insert(iterator position, const T& x);
```
For insertion in a given position. This insert function and those which follow take $O(n)$ time, where *n* is the number of elements that follow the inserted element; remember, these elements must be moved to make room for the inserted element(s). The returned iterator values refer to the inserted element. For example, the fragment

```
vector<int> v;
for (int k=10; k<15; k++) v.push_back(k);
vector<int>::iterator i = v.begin() + 1, j;
j = v.insert(i, 123);
copy(v.begin(), v.end(),       // See Section 1.9.
    ostream_iterator<int>(cout, " ")); cout << endl;
cout << "j refers to " << *j << endl;
```

produces the following output:

```
10 123 11 12 13 14
j refers to 123
```

```
void insert(iterator position, const_iterator first,
    const_iterator last);
```
Enables us to insert more than one new element at the same time. The elements to be inserted can be any valid range [*first*, *last*) of elements of the required type. Here is an example:

```
vector<int> v;
for (int k=0; k<5; k++) v.push_back(k);
int a[3] = {100, 200, 300};
v.insert(v.begin() + 1, a, a+3);
// Contents of v: 0 100 200 300 1 2 3 4
```

```
void insert (iterator position, size_type n,
   const T& x);
```
This is useful to insert several new elements, which are all equal to the third argument, *x*. For example:

```
vector<int> v;
for (int k=0; k<5; k++) v.push_back(k);
int initvalue = -1;
v.insert(v.begin() + 1, 4, initvalue);
// Contents of v: 0 -1 -1 -1 -1 1 2 3 4
```

```
void pop_back();
void erase(iterator position);
```
See Section 1.3.

```
void erase(iterator first, iterator last);
```
The elements in the range [*first*, *last*) are erased, as the following example illustrates:

```
vector<int> v;
for (int k=0; k<7; k++) v.push_back(10 * k);
   // Contents of v: 0, 10, 20, 30, 40, 50, 60
v.erase(v.begin()+2, v.begin()+5);
   // Contents of v: 0, 10, 50, 60
```

Both *erase* functions take $O(n)$ time, where *n* is the number of elements that follow the deleted elements. If we want to erase a number of consecutive vector elements, we should use a single call to the latter *erase* function because this is much faster than calling the former one repeatedly, deleting one element at a time.

Container member functions that only return information about containers, without changing them, are sometimes referred to as *accessors*.

3.4 Deques

As we have discussed several times, different container types are very similar in the way we use them. For example, each of the three container types *vector*, *deque* and *list* has a constructor that takes a repetition factor and a value as arguments, as this example illustrates:

```
vector<double> v(100, 12.34);
deque<double> D(100, 12.34);
list<double> L(100, 12.34);
```

Each of these three cases creates a sequence consisting of 100 occurrences of the value 12.34. As this example illustrates, we can shorten our discussion of deques and lists by restricting ourselves to subjects that are specific for these container types and referring to vectors for more general aspects.

Our discussions of *deques* in Sections 1.3 and 1.9 seem to imply that they have only advantages over vectors. They provide the member functions *push_front* and *pop_front*, in addition to the member functions provided by vectors. Since the most essential characteristic of a deque is its ability to grow and shrink at both ends, it seems natural to implement a deque as a doubly linked list. However, this is not the type of deque that is available in STL, since the latter, curiously enough, provide constant-time random access. You may wonder how such deques can be implemented. Figure 3.2 shows a model of such an implementation. The elements of this deque are located in fixed-size blocks. There is also an array, of pointers to these blocks. The shaded parts of the blocks are really in use, the white parts denote memory that has been allocated but has not yet been used.

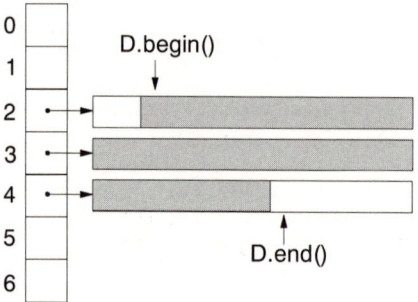

Figure 3.2 A possible implementation of deque D

The execution of

```
D.push_front(x);
```

implies that element *x* is placed just to the left of the position denoted by *D.begin()*. This insertion at the front causes the first arrow ↓ to move a little to the left. After this has happened several times, the first of the three blocks shown in the figure is full. A new block is then allocated, and a pointer to it is placed in position 1 of the array on the left. When this is also full, yet another block is allocated, pointed to by the array position 0. It seems that we have a problem when, after many more insertions, this is also full. However, we can solve this problem reasonably efficiently by reallocating the array of pointers. Now that there are five blocks, we allocate a much larger array of pointers and we use only the five elements in the middle, so that extensions are again possible at both ends. You can easily see that insertions at the end (instead of at the beginning) can be dealt with analogously.

Iterators referring to deque elements are not guaranteed to remain valid when elements are inserted. Recall that the same problem applies to vectors, as we have seen in Section 3.2. Because the blocks in Figure 3.2 have the same length, the address of a deque element can be computed in constant time; in other words, deques provide for random access. We can even use array notation, writing

    D[k]   instead of   *(D.begin() + k)

In view of the more complicated memory-allocation scheme, we may expect operations on deques to be slightly slower than those on vectors. This makes it logical that STL provides both vectors and deques: the constant-time *push_front* and *pop_front* functions are available for deques, not for vectors, but most operations that are available for both containers will probably be slightly faster for vectors than they are for deques.

No *reserve* and *capacity* functions (see Section 3.2) are available for deques, but there is a *size* member function, and, as usual

    D.size()   is equal to   D.end() - D.begin()

Most deque member functions behave in the same way as their vector counterparts; we will therefore not discuss them but rather refer to Section 3.3. Here are some declarations for deque member functions that are not available for vectors:

```
void push_front(const T& x);
void pop_front();
reference front();
```

For example, suppose we have a vector v and a deque D, both nonempty and with elements of the same type. Then the following fragment replaces the final element of v with the first element of a deque D, after which this first element of D is erased:

```
v.back() = D.front();
D.pop_front();
```

3.5 Lists

As we already know, an advantage of lists over vectors and deques is the possibility of inserting and deleting elements in any position in constant-time, but they have the disadvantage of not providing random access. An STL list can very well be implemented as a doubly-linked list, as shown in Figure 3.3. Since the nodes of this list contain links both to the next and to the previous nodes, the operations ++ and −−, applied to iterators, will be efficient, that is, they will take constant time. By contrast, moving from a node to a node that lies n positions further in the list will take $O(n)$ time.

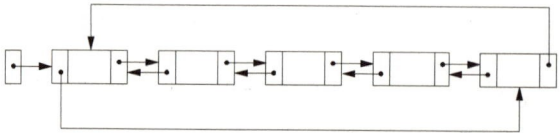

Figure 3.3 A doubly-linked list

To insert a node somewhere in the middle of the list, four pointer members of nodes have to be given appropriate values, since there must be two pointers (from its left and right neighbors) pointing to that node and two others pointing from that node to its neighbors. No other nodes have to be updated, which explains why insertion in any position is constant time. Deleting a node is equally efficient.

If nodes are inserted in a list, all iterators referring to nodes of that list remain valid, which, as we know, need not be the case with vectors and deques.

Many member functions, such as constructors and insert functions, can be used in the same way as with vectors and deques, but, as we have just been discussing, all list insertions take constant time. There is no subscripting operator [] for lists, since subscripting is associated with random-access iterators, while the list iterators are only bidirectional.

The *sort* and *unique* member functions

As we have seen in Section 1.4, the *sort* algorithm does not work with lists. Instead, there is a list member function *sort*. Another list-specific function is *unique*, which removes any consecutive duplicate elements. These two functions are declared in the class *list* as follows:

```
void sort();
void unique();
```

The following program demonstrates both functions:

```
// list1.cpp: The list member functions sort and unique.

#include <iostream>
#include <list>
using namespace std;

void out(char *s, const list<int> &L)
{  cout << s;
   copy(L.begin(), L.end(),
     ostream_iterator<int>(cout, " "));
   cout << endl;
}
```

```
int main()
{   list<int> L(5, 123);
    L.push_back(100);
    L.push_back(123);
    L.push_back(123);
    out("Initial contents: ", L);
    L.unique();
    out("After L.unique(): ", L);
    L.sort();
    out("After L.sort():    ", L);
    return 0;
}
```

As the output of this program shows, *unique* deals only with consecutive elements, resulting in two elements 123 in the result: one before and the other after the element 100.

```
Initial contents: 123 123 123 123 123 100 123 123
After L.unique(): 123 100 123
After L.sort():   100 123 123
```

If we had called the two member functions in the opposite order

```
L.sort(); L.unique();
```

the final result would have consisted of only two elements:

```
100 123
```

Splicing

Another list-specific operation is *splicing*, that is, moving one or more consecutive elements from one list to another, without allocating or deallocating memory for these elements. There are three *splice* member functions, which (inside the *list* class) can be declared as shown below. In the explaining comments, *L* and *M* are lists of the same type:

```
void splice(iterator position, list<T>& x);
```

If *i* is a valid iterator for *L*, the following statement inserts the contents of *M* before *i* in *L* and leaves *M* empty. This does *not* work if *L* and *M* are the same list:

```
L.splice(i, M);
```

```
void splice(iterator position, list<T>& x, iterator j);
```

If i is a valid iterator for L, and j likewise for M, the following statement removes the element to which j refers and inserts it before i. This also works if L and M are the same list:

```
L.splice(i, M, j);
```

```
void splice(iterator position, list<T>& x,
    iterator first, iterator last);
```

If i is a valid iterator for L and $[j1, j2)$ is a valid range in M, the following statement removes the elements of that range and inserts them before i in L. This also works if L and M are the same list:

```
L.splice(i, M, j1, j2);
```

We will demonstrate the last *splice* function to change the list as indicated in Figure 3.4.

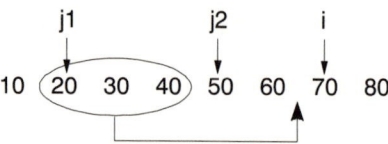

Figure 3.4 *Splicing*

The elements 20, 30, 40 of the sequence 10, 20, 30, 40, 50, 60, 70, 80 are moved to their new position between 60 and 70. The resulting sequence is

```
10 50 60 20 30 40 70 80
```

which is exactly the output produced by the following program:

```cpp
// splice.cpp: Splicing.
#include <iostream>
#include <list>
using namespace std;

int main()
{   list<int> L;
    list<int>::iterator i, j1, j2, j;
    for (int k = 10; k <= 80; k += 10)
    {   L.push_back(k);
        j = L.end();
        if (k == 20) j1 = --j; else
        if (k == 50) j2 = --j; else
        if (k == 70) i = --j;
    }
```

```
    L.splice(i, L, j1, j2);
    copy(L.begin(), L.end(),
        ostream_iterator<int>(cout, " "));
    cout << endl;
    return 0;
}
```

Note the statement

```
i = --j;
```

(and similar ones) in this program. We cannot replace this with

```
i = j - 1;
```

because the plus and minus operators are not defined for bidirectional iterators (see Section 1.9). The $--$ operator is required here because the iterator $j = L.end()$ refers to the position just after the most recent element, added by *push_back*. Instead of this solution with three if-statements, we could have used the *find* algorithm (see Section 1.5), replacing the above rather complicated for-loop with the following fragment:

```
for (int k = 10; k <= 80; k += 10)
    L.push_back(k);
j1 = find(L.begin(), L.end(), 20);
j2 = find(L.begin(), L.end(), 50);
i = find(L.begin(), L.end(), 70);
```

This fragment is quite acceptable for the short sequence used in this program, but the solution adopted in the complete program would have been more efficient than this fragment if the sequence had been very long.

Recall that 'algorithms' such as *find* are defined in the header *algorithm*, so that we may consider writing

```
#include <algorithm>
```

at the top of our program. Since, with BC5, this header is indirectly invoked by headers such as *vector* and *list*, we will omit this include line, assuming that other modern STL versions behave in the same way.

The list member function *remove*

If all list elements equal to a given value are to be deleted, the two-step approach, consisting of calls to the *remove* and *erase* algorithms, as discussed in Section 1.13, is not very efficient. It is much better to use the list member function *remove* for this purpose. This function is declared inside the *list* template class as follows:

```
void remove(const T& value);
```

This function is specific for lists; it is not available as member functions of vectors and deques. The following program shows that it is quite simple to use:

```cpp
// remove.cpp: The list member function remove.
#include <iostream>
#include <list>
using namespace std;

void out(const char *s, const list<int> &L)
{   cout << s;
    copy(L.begin(), L.end(),
        ostream_iterator<int>(cout, " "));
    cout << endl;
}

int main()
{   list<int> L;
    list<int>::iterator new_end;
    L.push_back(1); L.push_back(4); L.push_back(1);
    L.push_back(3); L.push_back(1); L.push_back(2);
    out("Initial sequence L:\n", L);
    L.remove(1);
    out("After L.remove(1):\n", L);
    return 0;
}
```

This program produces the following output:

```
Initial sequence L:
1 4 1 3 1 2
After L.remove(1):
4 3 2
```

The list member function *reverse*

The *list* class also provides a *reverse* function, declared in the class *list* as follows:

```cpp
void reverse();
```

This member function, available only for lists, not for vectors or deques, takes advantage of the ways lists are implemented. For a list *L* we therefore prefer the member-function call

```cpp
L.reverse();
```

to the following call of the *reverse* algorithm:

```cpp
reverse(L.begin(), L.end());
```

The list member function *merge*

Merging lists can be much more efficient than merging vectors or deques, since only links, not the list elements themselves, need to be copied. The *list* class contains the following declaration of a *merge* member function:

```
void merge(list<T>& x);
```

The following program demonstrates how to use this *merge* member function:

```
// lstmerge.cpp: The list member function merge.

#include <iostream>
#include <list>

using namespace std;

void out(const char *s, const list<int> &L)
{   cout << s;
    copy(L.begin(), L.end(),
        ostream_iterator<int>(cout, " "));
    cout << endl;
}

int main()
{   list<int> L1, L2, L3;
    list<int>::iterator new_end;
    L1.push_back(10); L1.push_back(20); L1.push_back(30);
    L2.push_back(15); L2.push_back(35);
    out("Initial sequence L1:\n", L1);
    out("Initial sequence L2:\n", L2);
    L1.merge(L2);
    out("After L1.merge(L2):\n", L1);
    return 0;
}
```

This program produces the following output:

```
Initial sequence L1:
10 20 30
Initial sequence L2:
15 35
After L1.merge(L2):
10 15 20 30 35
```

The last line shows the new list *L1*, while *L2* is empty. Although this *merge* function has the same name as the *merge* algorithm, the latter works entirely differently, as discussed in Section 1.7.

3.6 Vectors of Vectors

So far, *vector<int>* has been our favorite type in our sample programs. It goes without saying that we can replace *int* with other types, so we can also use *vector<double>*, *vector<char>*, and so on. We may wonder whether, instead of *int*, *double* and *char*, we can use more complex types, such as *vector<int>*, between the angular brackets. For example we may want to write

```
vector<vector<int> > A;
```

This is indeed possible, as the following program demonstrates:

```
// vecvec.cpp: A vector of vectors.

#include <iostream>
#include <vector>

using namespace std;

int main()
{   vector <int> v;
    v.push_back(8); v.push_back(9);
    vector<vector<int> > A;
    A.push_back(v);
    A.push_back(v);
    A.push_back(v);
    for (int i=0; i<3; i++)
    {   for (int j=0; j<2; j++)
            cout << A[i][j] << " ";
        cout << endl;
    }
    return 0;
}
```

This program uses a vector *A* of three elements, each of which is a vector of the two *int* values 8 and 9. We can regard this vector *A* as a two-dimensional array, or *matrix*, as the output of this program shows:

```
8 9
8 9
8 9
```

However, this practice may take considerably more memory than is actually required. It is quite usual for C and C++ programmers to use arrays of pointers instead of two-dimensional arrays. This suggests the use of a vector of pointers, as implemented in the following program, which produces the same output as the previous one:

```
// pointers.cpp: A vector of pointers.
#include <iostream>
#include <vector>
using namespace std;

typedef vector<int> vecint;

int main()
{  vector<vecint*> A;
   int a[2] = {8, 9};
   A.push_back(new vecint(a, a+2));
   A.push_back(new vecint(a, a+2));
   A.push_back(new vecint(a, a+2));
   for (int i=0; i<3; i++)
   {  for (int j=0; j<2; j++)
         cout << (*A[i])[j] << " ";
      cout << endl;
   }
   delete A[0]; delete A[1]; delete A[2];
   return 0;
}
```

Each vector element $A[i]$ is a pointer to a vector of two *int* elements, so that $*(A[i])$ is that vector itself, which explains the expression $*(A[i])[j]$ for the *int* values stored in A.

3.7 Avoiding Explicit Memory Allocation

As pointed out in Section 1.14, a notorious source of errors in complex programs is memory deallocation by means of *free* or *delete*. In the following functions, we must not omit these methods of deallocation. If we do, *memory leakage* will occur, since allocated memory is never deallocated.

```
void f(int n)
{  double *a;
   a = (double*)malloc(n * sizeof(double));
   ...                // Use a[0], ..., a[n-1].
   free(a);           // This prevents memory leakage.
}
```

or

```
void f(int n)
{  double *a;
   a = new double[n];
   ...                // Use a[0], ..., a[n-1].
   delete[] a;        // This prevents memory leakage.
}
```

We must not allocate the same block of memory more than once, and, if memory allocation is done conditionally, we must not deallocate the same memory unconditionally.

With STL, we can use the *vector* container to avoid the use of *malloc* or *new*. An advantage of this is the reduced risk of errors because we need not explicitly deallocate memory with *free* or *delete*. For example, instead of the above functions we can now write

```
#include <vector>
...
void f(int n)
{   vector<double> a(n);   // See Section 3.3.
    ... // use a[0], ..., a[n-1]
}
```

Deallocation is now taken care of by the destructor of the vector container.

Vector class members

We can also use vectors instead of explicitly allocated and deallocated arrays defined inside classes. For example, consider the following example of explicit allocation and deallocation:

```
class T {
public:
    T(int n){a = new double[n];}
    ~T(){delete[] a;}
    ...
    double *a;
};
```

This is another case in which *delete*[]*a* is required to avoid memory leakage. We omit such explicit memory deallocation if we use a vector constructor to allocate memory, as the following program shows:

```
// vecmem.cpp: A vector member of a class.
#include <iostream>
#include <vector>
#include <numeric>
using namespace std;

template <class eltype>
class objtype {
public:
    objtype(int n=0): a(n){}
    vector<eltype> a;
};
```

```
int main()
{   int n, i;
    double s=0;
    cout << "Enter n: ";
    cin >> n; // n is a positive integer
    objtype<double> x(n);
    for (i=0; i<n; i++) x.a[i] = i;
    s = accumulate(x.a.begin(), x.a.end(), s);
    cout << s << " = " << double(n-1)*n/2
         << endl;
    return 0;
}
```

The object x contains an array a of n values of type *double*, where n is entered by the user. We use the values 0, 1, ..., $n-1$ to fill this array, and then compute the sum of all array elements, using *accumulate*, as discussed in Section 2.1. In other words, we obtain

$$0 + 1 + 2 + ... + n - 1 = \frac{1}{2} n (n - 1)$$

This sum is computed in two ways, so we can easily check the result obtained by the *accumulate* algorithm. Here is a demonstration of this program to compute the value $\frac{1}{2} \times 100\,000 \times 99\,999 = 4\,999\,950\,000 = 4.99995 \times 10^9$:

```
Enter n: 100000
4.99995e+09 = 4.99995e+09
```

No copy constructors or assignment operators required

Another advantage of a vector class member is that copying and assignment of class objects will be done correctly without any need for a copy constructor or an assignment operator. The following program, based on the class we have just been using, illustrates this:

```
// simple.cpp: No copy constructor or
//     assignment operator required.
#include <iostream>
#include <vector>
#include <numeric>
using namespace std;

template <class eltype>
class objtype {
public:
    objtype(int n=0): a(n, 0){ }
    vector<eltype> a;
};
```

```
int main()
{  int i;
   double s;
   objtype<double> x(3), y(x);
   // Or, with assignment instead of initialization:
   //     objtype<double> x(3), y;
   //     y = x;
   x.a[1] = 123;
   copy(x.a.begin(), x.a.end(),
      ostream_iterator<double>(cout, " "));
   cout << endl;
   copy(y.a.begin(), y.a.end(),
      ostream_iterator<double>(cout, " "));
   cout << endl;
   return 0;
}
```

The output

```
0 123 0
0 0 0
```

of this program clearly demonstrates that the objects *x* and *y* are independent: the initial value (0, 0, 0) given to *y* is not destroyed by assigning a different value to *x*. If we had allocated memory in the *objtype* constructor using the *new* operator, the above initialization (using a 'deep' copy of *x* as the initial value) of *y* would have required a copy constructor. This is not required in the current version because the *vector* copy constructor supplied by STL is used. Similarly, we need not provide our own assignment operator, as indicated in the program text by a comment.

4

Associative Containers

4.1 Introduction

As we have seen in Section 2.5, there are four types of associative container: sets, multisets, maps and multimaps. Sets and multisets have two template parameters, while maps and multimaps have three, as the following fragments show:

```
template <class Key, class Compare>
class set { ...
};

template <class Key, class Compare>
class multiset { ...
};

template <class Key, class T, class Compare>
class map { ...
};

template <class Key, class T, class Compare>
class multimap { ...
};
```

You can find the complete definitions of these template classes in the headers *set* and *map*.

A note on portability

If you are using the older, HP version of STL, you should use the headers *set.h* and *map.h* for sets and maps but *multiset.h* and *multimap.h* for multisets and multimaps.

Compare and other function objects

Programmers new to STL may find function objects difficult to understand. This is partly due to some rather cryptic syntactic C++ constructs, which most programmers seldom use. In addition to our discussion in Section 1.12, let us deal with this important subject in some more detail. First, recall that the expression

```
int()
```

generates a constant integer 0, which implies that the following two statements are equivalent:

```
x = 0;
x = int();
```

For a non-standard type, say, *T*, the expression *T*() returns an object of type *T*, as the following program illustrates:

```
// gen_t.cpp: Generation of object T().
#include <iostream.h>

class T {
public:
   T(){i = 123;}
   int i;
};

int main()
{  int j = T().i;
   cout << j << endl; // Output: 123
   return 0;
}
```

Remember, if a type, such as *T* in the *main* function of the above example, is followed by a pair of parentheses without any argument, a *default constructor* for that type is called to generate an object. A default constructor has no (or only default) parameters. In this example, we supply such a default constructor for class *T*. If we did not, and did not supply any other constructor for *T* either, a default constructor, equivalent to *T*(){ }, would be generated.

Things are different if not a type, but an object is followed by a set of parentheses, which is the case if, with object *u* of type *U*, we use expressions such as these two:

```
u()
u(1, 2, 3)
```

Both expressions are illegal unless we define appropriate call-operators, written *operator*( ), as the following program shows:

```
// call_op.cpp: Two call-operators.

#include <iostream.h>

class U {
public:
    char operator()()
    {   return 'Q';
    }
    int operator()(int a, int b, int c)
    {   return a + b + c;
    }
};

int main()
{   U u;
    cout << "u() = " << u() << endl;
    cout << "u(1, 2, 3) = " << u(1, 2, 3) << endl;
    return 0;
}
```

This program produces the output

```
u() = Q
u(1, 2, 3) = 6
```

There are two call-operators in program *call_op.cpp*. The first takes no arguments and returns type *char*, while the second takes three arguments and returns type *int*.

The similarity between the expressions $T()$ and $u()$ in our last two programs is deceptive. Since T is a type and u is an object, $T()$ is actually more similar to u, where T is followed by parentheses and u is not; both $T()$ and u are objects. If we had defined call-operators for class T in the same way as we did for class U, the expressions

```
T()()
T()(1, 2, 3)
```

would have made sense.

In the following program, *LessThan* is a type like T in the above discussion, so that *LessThan*( ) is a function object and *LessThan*( )(2, 3) is a function call:

```
// lessthan.cpp: A LessThan function object.

#include <iostream.h>

class LessThan {
public:
    int operator()(int x, int y)
    {   return x < y;
    }
};

int main()
{   LessThan b;
    cout << "b(2, 3) = " << b(2, 3) << endl;
    cout << "LessThan()(2, 3) = " << LessThan()(2, 3)
         << endl;
    return 0;
}
```

This program produces the following output:

```
b(2, 3) = 1
LessThan()(2, 3) = 1
```

We have used the class *LessThan* to compare integers. We can generalize this class, defining a template class *less_than* to compare any two objects of the same type for which the operator < is defined, as the following program shows:

```
// lt_templ.cpp: A less-than template class.
#include <iostream.h>

template <class T>
class less_than {
public:
    int operator()(const T &x, const T &y)
    {   return x < y;
    }
};

int main()
{   less_than<int> b;
    cout << "b(2, 3) = " << b(2, 3) << endl;
    cout << "less_than<double>()(2.1, 2.2) = "
         << less_than<double>()(2.1, 2.2) << endl;
    return 0;
}
```

This program produces the following output:

```
b(2, 3) = 1
less_than<double>()(2.1, 2.2) = 1
```

In the last line, *less_than<double>* is a type and *less_than<double>*() is an object
of this type. Finally, the expression *less_than<double>*()(2.1, 2.2) is a call to the
member function *operator*() of this object.

All this may be helpful to understand expressions such as

```
settype S1(less<int>());
```

which we will encounter in the next section. In this definition of *S1*, the object
less<int>() (of type *less<int>*) is passed as an argument to the *settype* constructor.

4.2 Member Functions for Sets

There are three constructors for a set, which, inside the class, could have been
declared as follows:

```
set(const Compare& comp = Compare());  // 1 (default)

set(const value_type* first, const value_type* last,
    const Compare& comp = Compare());   // 2

set(const set<Key, Compare>& x);        // 3 (copy)
```

The identifier *Compare* in the above declarations denotes a template parameter,
which is a type. As we have seen in the previous section, this implies that
Compare() is an object. The following program uses each of these three constructors:

```
// setconst.cpp: Three set constructors

#include <iostream>
#include <set>

using namespace std;

typedef set<int, less<int> > settype;

void out(const char *s, const settype &S)
{   cout << s;
    copy(S.begin(), S.end(),
        ostream_iterator<int>(cout, " "));
    cout << endl;
}
```

```
int main()
{   int a[3] = {20, 10, 20};
    settype S1;                             // 1
    settype S2(a, a+3);                     // 2
    settype S3(S2);                         // 3
    out("S1: ", S1);
    out("S2: ", S2);
    out("S3: ", S3);
    return 0;
}
```

Although the range $[a, a+3)$ of three elements is given to construct $S2$, only the values of $a[0]$ and $a[1]$ are actually accepted as elements of the set $S2$, the third array element, $a[2]$, being equal to $a[0]$. The output of this program is:

```
S1:
S2: 10 20
S3: 10 20
```

The compare argument is omitted, so the default parameter value *less<int>*() applies in the definitions of $S1$ and $S2$. In other words, we would have had exactly the same effect if we had written:

```
settype S1(less<int>());                    // 1
settype S2(a, a+3, less<int>());            // 2
```

Note that the third set constructor (indicated by the comment // 3) is a copy constructor, which can be used not only to initialize variables but also to copy arguments (in the case of non-reference parameters) and in return-statements.

The following two member functions return the compare function object. Both types *key_compare* and *value_compare* are defined as the *Compare* parameter of the template class.

```
key_compare key_comp() const;
value_compare value_comp() const;
```

Although very impractical, the following example shows a possible use:

```
cout << "settype::value_compare()(2, 3) = "
     << settype::value_compare()(2, 3) << endl;
```

If we insert this very strange statement in the main function of program *setconst.cpp*, it would produce the following output line:

```
settype::value_compare()(2, 3) = 1
```

The following member functions are similar to those for sequence containers:

```
iterator begin() const;
iterator end() const;
reverse_iterator rbegin() const;
reverse_iterator rend() const;
bool empty() const;
size_type size() const;
size_type max_size();
void swap(set<Key, Compare>& x);
```

In program *setconst.cpp* we have $S1.size() = 0$ and $S2.size() = 2$. As usual, the function *max_size()* returns a very large value, such as 3 214 748 364.

As discussed in Section 2.10 for maps, there is an *insert* function for sets that returns a pair consisting of an iterator and a *bool* value. It is declared as follows:

```
pair<iterator, bool> insert(const value_type& x);
```

The return value provides both an iterator referring to the position of the value x after insertion in the set, and a *bool* value which is *true* if insertion really has taken place or *false* if x was already present in the set.

The second *insert* function takes an iterator as its first parameter; it is used as a hint, indicating the position after which the new value is to be inserted. Insertion is fastest if the new value can be inserted immediately after the position indicated by this first argument. This *insert* function is declared as follows:

```
iterator insert(iterator position, const value_type& x);
```

Finally, there is an *insert* function to insert a whole range of values.

```
void insert(const value_type* first,
   const value_type* last);
```

We can use this if we are given a range of (consecutive) array elements and we want to insert these in a set, as the following program shows:

```
// insrange.cpp: Inserting a range of values.
#include <iostream>
#include <set>
using namespace std;

int main()
{   int a[3] = {20, 10, 20};
    set<int, less<int> > S;
    S.insert(a, a+2);
    copy(S.begin(), S.end(),
       ostream_iterator<int>(cout, " "));
    cout << endl;       // Output 10 20
    return 0;
}
```

There are three functions to erase set elements:

```
void erase(iterator position);              // 1
size_type erase(const key_type& x);         // 2
void erase(iterator first, iterator last);  // 3
```

If we know the position of the set element to be erased, the first of these functions is recommended. If only the value of that element is known, we use the second; this returns the number of erased elements, which is normally 1 but could be 0 if the given value *x* is not found in the set. The third of the above three functions erases a whole range [*first*, *last*) of values. It follows that we can erase all elements of set *S*, making *S* empty, by writing

```
S.erase(S.begin(), S.end());
```

Since set elements are unique (so that no two elements can be equal), the *count* function, declared as

```
size_type count(const key_type& x) const;
```

will return either 0 or 1. For example, if *S* is a set of integers, *S.count*(123) is equal to 1 if 123 belongs to S; otherwise *S.count*(123) is equal to 0.

The following three functions search the set for a given value *x*:

```
iterator find(const key_type& x) const;
iterator lower_bound(const key_type& x) const;
iterator upper_bound(const key_type& x) const;
```

As usual, after executing

```
i = S.find(x);
```

the iterator *i* is equal to *S.end*() if *x* is not found; otherwise **i* is equal to *x*. To find the smallest range [*i, j*) of *S* containing a given value *x*, we can write

```
i = S.lower_bound(x);
j = S.upper_bound(x);
```

For example, suppose that *S* consists of the integers 30, 40 and 50. The table below then shows the values of *i* and *j* for several values of *x*. As the values $x = 25, 35, 45$ and 55 illustrate, the function calls *S.lower_bound*(x) and *S.upper_bound*(x) return equal iterator values if *S* does not contain *x*. In contrast, the values 30, 40 and 50 for *x* show that these iterator values are different if *S* contains *x*:

x	$i = S.lower\_bound(x);$	$j = S.upper\_bound(x);$
25	$*i = 30$	$*j = 30$
30	$*i = 30$	$*j = 40$
35	$*i = 40$	$*j = 40$
40	$*i = 40$	$*j = 50$
45	$*i = 50$	$*j = 50$
50	$*i = 50$	$j = S.end()$
55	$i = S.end()$	$j = S.end()$

The function *equal_range* returns the above pair (i, j) in a single call. This function is declared below:

```
pair<iterator, iterator> equal_range(const key_type& x)
   const;
```

Instead of calling the *lower_bound* and *upper_bound* functions individually, as we did above by the statements

```
i = S.lower_bound(x);
j = S.upper_bound(x);
```

it is more efficient to find *i* and *j* by using *equal_range*, as the following program shows:

```
// eqrange.cpp: The equal_range member function.

#include <set>
#include <iostream>

using namespace std;

int main()
{  typedef set<int, less<int> > settype;
   typedef settype::iterator iterator;
   settype S;
   S.insert(30);
   S.insert(40);
   S.insert(50);
   pair<iterator, iterator> P(0, 0);
   iterator i, j;
   int x = 30;
   P = S.equal_range(x);
   i = P.first; j = P.second;
   cout << *i << " " << *j << endl; // Output: 30 40
   return 0;
}
```

4.3 Set Unions and Intersections

In this section we will deal with the well-known mathematical operations of forming the intersection and the union of two sets, as illustrated by Figure 4.1.

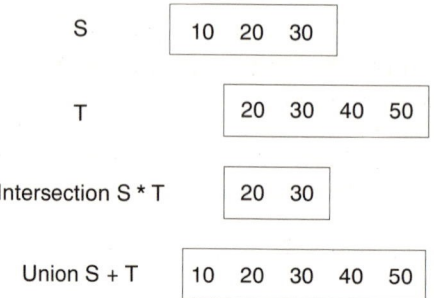

Figure 4.1 *Intersection and union of two sets*

Let us use the operators * and + for the intersection and union operations, while these are normally denoted by the symbols $\cap$ and $\cup$ in mathematics. With two given sets S and T, the intersection $S * T$ is defined as the set consisting of all elements that belong both to S and to T, and the union $S + T$ is the set consisting of all elements that belong to S or T (or to both). The following program shows how we can define such * and + operators for sets:

```
// intuni1.cpp: Intersection and union of sets.
#include <iostream>
#include <set>
#include <algorithm>
using namespace std;
typedef set<int, less<int> > settype;

settype operator*(const settype &S, const settype &T)
{   settype I;   // Intersection
    set_intersection(S.begin(), S.end(),
                     T.begin(), T.end(),
                     inserter(I, I.begin()));
    return I;
}

settype operator+(const settype &S, const settype &T)
{   settype U;   // Union
    set_union(S.begin(), S.end(),
              T.begin(), T.end(),
              inserter(U, U.begin()));
    return U;
}
```

```
void out(const char *s, const settype &S)
{   cout << s;
    copy(S.begin(), S.end(),
        ostream_iterator<int>(cout, " "));
    cout << endl;
}

int main()
{   int aS[3] = {10, 20, 30}, aT[4] = {20, 30, 40, 50};
    settype S(aS, aS + 3),
            T(aT, aT + 4);
    out("S =      ", S);
    out("T =      ", T);
    out("S * T = ", S * T);
    out("S + T = ", S + T);
    return 0;
}
```

Based on Figure 4.1, this program produces the following output:

```
S =      10 20 30
T =      20 30 40 50
S * T = 20 30
S + T = 10 20 30 40 50
```

It is an instructive exercise to define the operators * and + in terms of the *insert* member function instead of the algorithms *set_intersection* and *set_union*. Such versions are listed below; if they replace those in the above program, this will produce exactly the same output:

```
// Two functions that we might use if the algorithms
// set_intersection and set_union did not exist:
settype operator*(const settype &S, const settype &T)
{   settype I;   // Intersection
    settype::iterator
        firstS = S.begin(), lastS = S.end(),
        firstT = T.begin(), lastT = T.end(),
        i = I.begin();
    while (firstS != lastS && firstT != lastT)
    {   if (*firstS < *firstT) ++firstS; else
        if (*firstT < *firstS) ++firstT; else
        {   i = I.insert(i, *firstS++);
            ++firstT;
        }
    }
    return I;
}
```

```
settype operator+(const settype &S, const settype &T)
{   settype U;   // Union
    settype::iterator
        firstS = S.begin(), lastS = S.end(),
        firstT = T.begin(), lastT = T.end(),
        i = U.begin();
    while (firstS != lastS && firstT != lastT)
        i = U.insert(i,
            (*firstS < *firstT ? *firstS++ : *firstT++));
    while (firstS != lastS) i = U.insert(i, *firstS++);
    while (firstT != lastT) i = U.insert(i, *firstT++);
    return U;
}
```

It goes without saying that the original, simple versions are to be preferred to these much more complex ones.

It is by no means necessary to use * and + operators for intersection and union operations, as the following, equivalent program shows; this version is more efficient since it avoids passing sets as return values of functions:

```
// intunio2.cpp: Intersection and union of sets.
#include <iostream>
#include <set>
#include <algorithm>
using namespace std;
typedef set<int, less<int> > settype;

void out(const char *s, const settype &S)
{   cout << s;
    copy(S.begin(), S.end(),
        ostream_iterator<int>(cout, " "));
    cout << endl;
}

int main()
{   int aS[3] = {10, 20, 30}, aT[4] = {20, 30, 40, 50};
    settype S(aS, aS + 3), T(aT, aT + 4), prod, sum;
    out("S =      ", S); out("T =      ", T);
    set_intersection(S.begin(), S.end(),
        T.begin(), T.end(), inserter(prod, prod.begin()));
    out("S * T = ", prod);
    set_union(S.begin(), S.end(),
        T.begin(), T.end(),inserter(sum, sum.begin()));
    out("S + T = ", sum);
    return 0;
}
```

The algorithms *set_intersection* and *set_union* are not restricted to set containers but they also apply to other sorted structures, as we will see in Section 7.3.8.

4.4 Differences Between Multisets and Sets

We have discussed sets and multisets in Section 2.6, and it may be worthwhile to have another look at the program *multiset.cpp* of that section. Recall that each element of a set is unique, while multisets can contain several elements that are equal. Because of this difference, one of the *insert* functions for multisets is simpler than its counterpart for sets. As we have seen in Section 4.2, there is an *insert* function for sets which is declared as

```
pair<iterator, bool> insert(const value_type& x); // set
```

Recall that this function returns a pair consisting of an iterator and a *bool* value which is *false* if the insert operation fails because it was already in the set. In contrast, inserting a new element in a multiset always succeeds, so that no *bool* result is required. The corresponding multiset *insert* function therefore simply returns an iterator, as this declaration shows:

```
iterator insert(const value_type& x); // multiset
```

All other member functions for multisets have declarations identical with those for sets, apart from the obvious differences in the names *multiset* and *set* occurring in these declarations. The function *find*, if successful, returns the iterator referring to the *first* element that has the given value, as the following program illustrates:

```cpp
// msfind.cpp: Multiset find.
#include <iostream>
#include <set>

using namespace std;

typedef multiset<int, less<int> > multisettype;
typedef multisettype::iterator Iterator;

void out(Iterator first, Iterator last)
{  for (Iterator i = first; i != last; ++i)
      cout << *i << " ";
   cout << endl;
}

int main()
{  int a[5] = {10, 20, 20, 20, 30};
   multisettype M(a, a + 5);
   out(M.begin(), M.end());
   cout << "Subrange starting at element 20:\n";
   out(M.find(20), M.end());
   return 0;
}
```

This program produces the output

```
10 20 20 20 30
Subrange starting at element 20:
20 20 20 30
```

which shows that the iterator returned by the *find* function refers to the first element that is found. If the call *M.find*(20) had been unsuccessful because of no element 20 being stored in multiset *M*, this call would have returned *M.end*( ).

4.5 Maps

There are three map constructors, declared as

```
map(const Compare& comp = Compare());                          // 1
map(const value_type* first, const value_type* last,
    const Compare& comp = Compare());                          // 2
map(const map<Key, T, Compare>& x);                            // 3
```

The following program shows how each of them can be used:

```
// mapcstr.cpp: Map constructors
#include <iostream>
#include <map>
using namespace std;
typedef map<int, double, less<int> > maptype;
typedef pair<int, double> Pair;

int main()
{  pair<int, double> a[3] =
   {  Pair(20, 1.5),
      Pair(800, 0.3),
      Pair(3, 0.2)
   };
   maptype MA;                // 1 (start with empty map)
   maptype MB(a, a + 3);      // 2 (use array to initialize)
   maptype MC(MB);            // 3 (use MB to initialize)
   cout << MC[800] << endl;   // MC[800] = MB[800] = 0.3
   return 0;
}
```

The initialization of map *MB* is much simpler than that of the array *a* of pairs, on which it is based. Thanks to the copy constructor (marked // 3 at the beginning of this section), we can define map *MC* as a copy of *MB*.

The subscripting operator [ ] is very useful. We can use it not only to extract data from a map, as we did with *MC* in our last program, but also to insert data.

For example, instead of by using array *a* in that program, we could have inserted data in *MB* in a much easier way, as the following program shows:

```
// mapsubs.cpp: Map subscripting.
#include <iostream>
#include <map>
using namespace std;

typedef map<int, double, less<int> > maptype;

int main()
{  maptype MB;
   MB[20] = 1.5;
   MB[800] = 0.3;
   MB[3] = 0.2;
   cout << MB[800] << endl; // 0.3
   return 0;
}
```

Subscripting is a mapping from keys (20, 800 and 3) to associated values (1.5, 0.3 and 0.2), as Figure 4.2 illustrates.

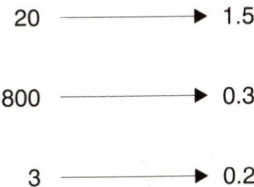

Figure 4.2 *Mapping from keys to values*

With normal array subscripting, we use consecutive subscripts 0, 1, 2, ..., which need not be stored themselves because the array elements are stored contiguously. By contrast, both keys and associated values of maps are stored in a balanced binary search tree, as shown in Figure 4.3.

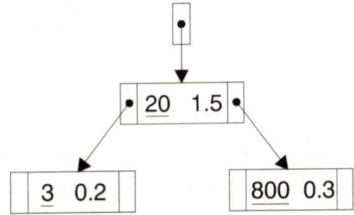

Figure 4.3 *Balanced binary search tree representing a map*

Binary search trees can be searched for the keys (underlined in Figure 4.3) because of the way the tree is constructed: for every node, all keys in its left subtree are less than the key in the node itself, while all keys in its right subtree are greater than that key.

Map *insert* member functions

Instead of using subscripting, we can insert map elements by means of three *insert* member functions, declared as follows:

```
pair<iterator, bool> insert(const value_type& x);
iterator insert(iterator position, const value_type& x);
void insert(const value_type* first,
    const value_type* last);
```

This is similar to the *insert* functions for sets, discussed in Section 4.2, but the type *value_type* is more complex because each element consists of a pair (key, associated value). As we have seen in the program *mapcstr.cpp*, we can use the *pair<int, double>* constructor to construct such a pair. For example, instead of

```
MB[800] = 0.3;
```

we can write

```
M.insert(pair<int, double>(k, x));
```

ignoring the value returned by this *insert* function. However, this insert function fails if the key is already present in the map.

The following program shows how this return value can be used. It forms a map consisting of only one element (800, 0.3). An attempt to replace this element with the element (800, 0.7) fails because this has the same key:

```
// mapins.cpp: Value returned by map insert function.

#include <iostream>
#include <map>
using namespace std;

typedef map<int, double, less<int> > maptype;
typedef maptype::iterator Iterator;

void MyInsert(maptype &M, int k, double x)
{  pair<Iterator, bool>
      P = M.insert(pair<int, double>(k, x));
   Iterator i = P.first;
   bool b = P.second;
```

```
      cout << "After attempt to insert (" << k << ", " << x
          << "), returning P = (i, b):\n";
      cout << "(*i).first = " << (*i).first << endl;
      cout << "(*i).second = " << (*i).second << endl;
      cout << "b = " << b << endl << endl;
  }

  int main()
  { maptype M;
    MyInsert(M, 800, 0.3);
    MyInsert(M, 800, 0.7);
    return 0;
  }
```

This program produces the following output:

```
After attempt to insert (800, 0.3), returning P = (i, b):
(*i).first = 800
(*i).second = 0.3
b = 1

After attempt to insert (800, 0.7), returning P = (i, b):
(*i).first = 800
(*i).second = 0.3
b = 0
```

Each insert operation in the program returns a pair (i, b), where i is an iterator referring to the inserted element and b is a *bool* value indicating whether insertion was successful. The last two lines of the above output show that the element (800, 0.7) was not inserted: the value of (*i).*second* is still 0.3, not 0.7, and b is equal to 0 (= *false*). If we insist on inserting the element (k, x), replacing any existing element with the same key k, we simply write

```
M[k] = x;
```

In the function *MyInsert*, we could have used the expression

```
maptype::value_type(k, x)
```

instead of

```
pair<int, double>(k, x)
```

You may wonder why we did not use the expression

```
i->first
```

instead of

```
(*i).first
```

Such a simplification would indeed be possible if *i* were a pointer, but it is an iterator, for which the operator −> is not defined.

To delete map elements, we can use three *erase* functions, declared as follows:

```
void erase(iterator position);
size_type erase(const key_type& x);
void erase(iterator first, iterator last);
```

These functions are similar to those for sets, so we need not discuss them in detail. This also applies to the functions *find*, *count*, *lower_bound* and *upper_bound*.

4.6 Multimaps

As discussed in Section 2.7, multimaps differ from maps in that they admit two or more elements with equal keys. Figure 4.4 shows a possible representation of a multimap. This tree could not represent a map because there are two elements that have the same key, equal to 3.

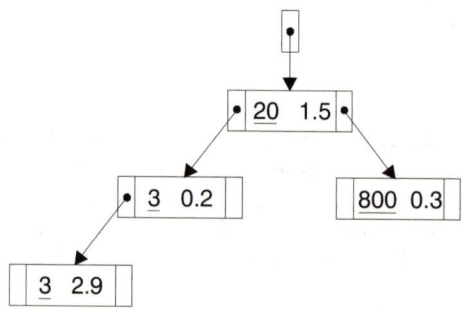

Figure 4.4 Balanced binary search tree representing a multimap

Multimap constructors are similar to those of maps, so we shall not discuss them explicitly, but rather focus on the points in which multimaps differ from maps.

The convenient subscripting operator, available for maps, is not available for multimaps. For example, we cannot replace the line

```
D.insert(mmtype::value_type("Johnson, J.", 12345));
```

found in the program *multimap.cpp* in Section 2.7, with this one:

```
D["Johnson, J."] = 12345; // ???
```

The *insert* and *erase* member functions for multimaps are declared as follows:

```
iterator insert(const value_type& x);
iterator insert(iterator position, const value_type& x);
void insert(const value_type* first,
            const value_type* last);

void erase(iterator position);
size_type erase(const key_type& x);
void erase(iterator first, iterator last);
```

These functions are similar to their counterparts for maps, except for the first *insert* function, which simply returns an iterator referring to the inserted element. Since insertion succeeds also if there is already an element with the same key, there is no need for a returned *bool* value indicating whether insertion was successful.

We may wonder in which order elements with equal keys are inserted in a multimap. The following program shows very clearly how this is done:

```
// mmapins.cpp: Multimap insertion.

#include <iostream>
#include <map>

using namespace std;

typedef multimap<int, double, less<int> > multimaptype;
typedef multimaptype::iterator Iterator;

void MyInsert(multimaptype &M, int k, double x)
{  Iterator i = M.insert(pair<int, double>(k, x));
   cout << (*i).first << " " << (*i).second;
   // Equivalent to:
   // cout << k << " " << x;
   cout << " inserted\n";
}

int main()
{  multimaptype M;
   MyInsert(M, 800, 0.3);
   MyInsert(M, 800, 0.7);
   MyInsert(M, 800, 0.5);
   MyInsert(M, 100, 1.9);
   MyInsert(M, 800, 0.6);
   cout << "Multimap traversal:\n";
   for (Iterator i = M.begin(); i != M.end(); ++i)
      cout << (*i).first << " " << (*i).second << endl;
   return 0;
}
```

The output of this program shows that the order of elements with equal keys is the same as the order in which they were inserted. By contrast, different keys appear in increasing order, regardless of the order in which they are inserted:

```
800 0.3 inserted
800 0.7 inserted
800 0.5 inserted
100 1.9 inserted
800 0.6 inserted
Multimap traversal:
100 1.9
800 0.3
800 0.7
800 0.5
800 0.6
```

The second of the above three *erase* functions (with one argument, a key) erases all elements with the given key and it returns the number of elements that were erased. For example, in the program *mmapins.cpp*, if we insert the lines

```
int n = M.erase(800);
cout << n << " elements erased\n";
```

immediately after the five calls to *MyInsert*, the output will be as follows:

```
800 0.3 inserted
800 0.7 inserted
800 0.5 inserted
100 1.9 inserted
800 0.6 inserted
4 elements erased
Multimap traversal:
100 1.9
```

4.7 A Concordance

We will now develop an application based on the notions of map and set as well as on the *string* class discussed in Section 2.12. We will write a program, called a *concordance*, which accepts any textfile as input, and, for each word in the file, shows the numbers of all lines on which that word occurs. If a word occurs more than once on the same line, the number of that line will appear only once for that word in the output, and the words will appear in alphabetical order. A word is defined as a sequence of consecutive letters. Capital letters will be converted to lower case. For example, let us use the first program of this book, copied below from Section 1.1, as an input file:

```
// ftempl.cpp: A template function.
#include <iostream.h>

template <class T>
T f(T x)
{   T x2 = 2 * x;
    return x2 + (x * x + 1)/x2;
}

int main()
{   cout << f(5.0) << endl << f(5) << endl;
    return 0;
}
```

This input file clearly shows that all kinds of characters may occur in it. With this file as input, our concordance program will produce the output shown in the following demonstration:

```
Enter name of input file: ftempl.cpp
a                1
class            4
cout             11
cpp              1
endl             11
f                5 11
ftempl           1
function         1
h                2
include          2
int              10
iostream         2
main             10
return           7 12
t                4 5 6
template         1 4
x                5 6 7
```

Thanks to the *map* container of STL, we can store all words in a balanced binary search tree (which makes searching a very fast operation), without actually programming such a tree. Each node of this tree contains both a word (acting as a key) and a set of line numbers. In STL terminology, each map element consists of a pair (*first*, *second*), where

> *first*   = a word, of type *string*
> *second* = a set of line numbers, of type *set<int>*

We also use the type *string* for the name of the input file, as the following program shows:

```cpp
// concord.cpp: A concordance based on maps,
//     sets and strings.

#include <iostream>
#include <fstream>
#include <iomanip>
#include <ctype.h>
#include <string>
#include <set>
#include <map>
using namespace std;

typedef set<int, less<int> > settype;
typedef map<string, settype, less<string> > maptype;

bool wordread(ifstream &ifstr, string &word,
    int &linenr)
{   char ch;
    // scan for first letter:
    for (;;)
    {   ifstr.get(ch);
        if (ifstr.fail()) return false;
        if (isalpha(ch)) break;
        if (ch == '\n') linenr++;
    }
    word = "";
    // scan for first non-alpha character:
    do
    {   word += tolower(ch);
        ifstr.get(ch);
    }   while (!ifstr.fail() && isalpha(ch));
    if (ifstr.fail()) return false;
    ifstr.putback(ch); // ch may be '\n'
    return true;
}

int main()
{   maptype M;
    maptype::iterator im;
    settype::iterator is, isbegin, isend;
    string inpfilename, word;
    ifstream ifstr;
    int linenr = 1;
    cout << "Enter name of input file: ";
    cin >> inpfilename;
    ifstr.open(inpfilename.c_str());
    if (!ifstr)
    {    cout << "Cannot open input file.\n"; exit(1);
    }
```

```
      while (wordread(ifstr, word, linenr))
      {   im = M.find(word);
          if (im == M.end())
              im = M.insert(maptype::value_type(word,
                  settype())).first;
          (*im).second.insert(linenr);
      }
      for (im = M.begin(); im != M.end(); im++)
      {   cout << setiosflags(ios::left) << setw(15)
              << (*im).first.c_str();
          isbegin = (*im).second.begin();
          isend = (*im).second.end();
          for (is=isbegin; is != isend; is++)
              cout << " " << *is;
          cout << endl;
      }
      return 0;
  }
```

The function *wordread* skips irrelevant characters, increases the line counter, if
required, and then reads one word. Although this function comprises a substantial
portion of the program, we will not discuss this in detail, since it is not closely
related to STL. The following fragment builds the complete map containing all
essential data:

```
  while (wordread(ifstr, word, linenr))
  {   im = M.find(word);
      if (im == M.end())
          im = M.insert(maptype::value_type(word,
              settype())).first;
      (*im).second.insert(linenr);
  }
```

If possible, the call *wordread(ifstr, word, linenr)* reads the next word from the
stream *ifstr*. It also increases the variable *linenr* if, just before that word, a newline
character has been read. The function *wordread* returns *true* if a word has been
read, and *false* if the end of the input file has been encountered. We then use the
find member function to search the map for the word just read. We now distinguish
two cases: found and not found. Recall that each map element consists of both a
word and a set of line numbers. If the word is found in the map, the current line
number is inserted in this set, as we will see in a moment. If it is not found, the
returned map iterator *im* is equal to *M.end( )*, and we first have to insert a new map
element, containing the word in question and an empty set. We do this by executing
a rather complicated two-line statement, which is of the following form:

```
  im = M.insert(xxx).first;
```

This call to *insert* returns a pair (*iterator, true*) because we know that the key was not yet present in the map. The iterator value of this pair, indicating the position of the newly inserted element, is stored in the variable *im*. In the above form, *xxx* stands for a pair (*k, d*), where *k* is the word in question and *d* is the empty set, denoted here by *settype*( ). Recall that this expression invokes the default constructor of *settype*, the type of the sets we are using. For this pair (*k, d*) = *xxx* in the above form, we actually write

```
maptype::value_type(word, settype())
```

Recall that we have discussed *value_type* in Sections 2.7, 2.10 and 3.1. Now in either of the two cases just mentioned, *im* refers to a map element that contains the word in question as (**im*).*first*. The current line number is then inserted in the corresponding set (**im*).*second* as follows:

```
(*im).second.insert(linenr);
```

5

Container Adaptors

5.1 Stacks

A *stack* is a data structure that admits only two operations to modify its size: *push*, to insert an element at the end, and *pop*, to delete an element at the end. In other words, a stack is based on the principle of Last In First Out (LIFO). Besides *push* and *pop*, there are also the member functions *empty* and *size*, with their usual meaning, and *top* (instead of *back*) for access to the final element.

We can represent a stack by each of the three STL sequence containers vector, deque and list. A stack is therefore not an entirely new container type, but rather a special version of a vector, a deque or a list, which explains the term container *adaptor*.

For example, let us use a stack to read a sequence of integers and to display them in reverse order. Any nonnumeric character will act as a code for 'end of input'. In the following program this stack is represented by a vector, but it also works if we replace all occurrences of *vector* with *deque* or *list*. This program also demonstrates the use of the member functions *empty*, *top* and *size*.

```
// stack1.cpp: Using a stack to read a number sequence
//    of arbitrary length and to display this sequence
//    in reverse order.

#include <iostream>
#include <vector>
#include <stack>
using namespace std;
```

```
int main()
{   stack <int, vector<int> > S;
    int x;
    cout <<
        "Enter some integers, followed by a letter:\n";
    while (cin >> x) S.push(x);
    while (!S.empty())
    {   x = S.top();
        cout << "Size: " << S.size()
            << "      Element at the top: " << x << endl;
        S.pop();
    }
    return 0;
}
```

According to the Draft C++ Standard, the *stack* template has two arguments, as this program line shows:

```
stack <int, vector<int> > S;
```

With the original HP STL version the first of these arguments does not occur, so you should replace this line with

```
stack <vector<int> > S;
```

if you are using this (older) version of STL.

After some integers, entered by the user, have been pushed onto the stack, the program repeatedly displays both the stack size and the element to be popped from the stack, as this demonstration shows:

```
Enter some integers, followed by a letter:
10 20 30 A
Size: 3      Element at the top: 30
Size: 2      Element at the top: 20
Size: 1      Element at the top: 10
```

We cannot use iterators for stacks, let alone traverse them. The stack container provides the assignment operator = and the comparison operators == and <. As discussed in Section 2.8, this implies that the other four comparison operators are also available. The operator < performs a lexicographic comparison, as the following program demonstrates:

```
// stackcmp.cpp: Stack assignments and comparisons.
#include <iostream>
#include <vector>
#include <stack>
using namespace std;
```

```cpp
int main()
{   stack <int, vector<int> > S, T, U;
    S.push(10); S.push(20); S.push(30);
    cout << "Pushed onto S: 10 20 30\n";
    T = S;
    cout << "After T = S; we have ";
    cout << (S == T ? "S == T" : "S != T") << endl;
    U.push(10); U.push(21);
    cout << "Pushed onto U: 10 21\n";
    cout << "We now have ";
    cout << (S < U ? "S < U" : "S >= U") << endl;
    return 0;
}
```

This program produces the following output:

```
Pushed onto S: 10 20 30
After T = S; we have S == T
Pushed onto U: 10 21
We now have S < U
```

Figure 5.1 illustrates the last comparison.

Stack S   `<`   Stack U

Figure 5.1 *Lexicographical comparison of stacks*

The elements at the bottom are compared first. Since these are both 10, the second lowest elements, 20 and 21, are compared. We have S < U because 20 < 21. This is similar to the comparison of strings, where we start with the first characters instead of the elements at the bottom of the stacks.

Recall that the definition of the operators == and < implies that the operators !=, >, <= and >= are also available, as we have discussed in Section 2.8.

It is interesting to note that the *top* member function returns a reference, which enables us to modify the top of a nonempty stack without performing a pop and a push operation. For example, we can simply write

```cpp
S.top() = 15;
```

instead of

```cpp
S.pop();
S.push(15);
```

5.2 Queues

A *queue* is a data structure in which we can insert elements at one end, the back, and remove them from the opposite end, the front. We can inspect (and modify) the elements at the front and at the back, as Figure 5.2 illustrates.

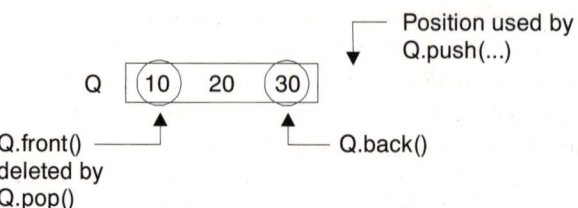

Figure 5.2 A queue

Unlike a stack, we cannot represent a queue by a vector, because this does not provide the *pop_front* operation. For example, we cannot write

```
queue <int, vector<int> > Q;  // Error
```

This line will be correct if we replace *vector* with either *deque* or *list*. The following program shows that the queue member functions *push* and *pop* work as indicated in Figure 5.2.

```
// queue.cpp: Using a queue; a demonstration of
//       the member functions push, pop, back and front.

#include <iostream>
#include <list>
#include <queue>

using namespace std;

int main()
{  queue <int, list<int> > Q;
   Q.push(10); Q.push(20); Q.push(30);
   cout << "After pushing 10, 20 and 30:\n";
   cout << "Q.front() = " << Q.front() << endl;
   cout << "Q.back()  = " << Q.back() << endl;
   Q.pop();
   cout << "After Q.pop():\n";
   cout << "Q.front() = " << Q.front() << endl;
   return 0;
}
```

The output of this program is

```
After pushing 10, 20 and 30:
Q.front() = 10
Q.back()  = 30
After Q.pop():
Q.front() = 20
```

Curiously enough, the header to be used for queues is *stack.h* with HP STL, while it is *queue* with the Draft C++ Standard (see also the table in Section 1.2). Also, the number of template arguments differs; we will not discuss this in detail, since this difference is the same as it is with stacks, as discussed in the previous section.

The queue member functions *empty* and *size* are similar to those of the stack container, and so are the assignment and comparison operators. Comparison starts at the front elements; if these are equal the next elements are compared, and so on.

5.3 Priority Queues

A *priority queue* is a data structure in which, as long as it is not empty, only the largest element can be retrieved. As with stacks, the most important member functions are *push*, *pop* and *top*. The following program uses these functions:

```
// prqueue.cpp: A priority queue; a demonstration of
//   the member functions push, pop, empty and top.
#include <iostream>
#include <vector>
#include <functional>
#include <queue>

using namespace std;

int main()
{  priority_queue <int, vector<int>, less<int> > P;
   int x;
   P.push(123); P.push(51); P.push(1000); P.push(17);
   while (!P.empty())
   {  x = P.top();
      cout << "Retrieved element: " << x << endl;
      P.pop();
   }
   return 0;
}
```

This program produces the following output, in which the numbers appear in descending order:

```
Retrieved element: 1000
Retrieved element: 123
Retrieved element: 51
Retrieved element: 17
```

Since it is essential that elements can be compared, the *priority_queue* template takes a third argument, as shown by this definition of priority queue *P*:

```
priority_queue <int, vector<int>, less<int> > P;
```

If we want to retrieve the elements in increasing order, we simply replace *less<int>* with *greater<int>*. With HP STL, the first template argument should be omitted, and the header to be used is *stack.h* instead of *queue*.

To show that we can specify any ordering we like, let us use yet another example, in which the elements are retrieved in increasing order of the final digits of the integers stored in the priority queue:

```
// lastdig.cpp: A priority queue; P.top() is the element
//    whose last digit is less than (or equal to) that of
//    the other elements.

#include <iostream>
#include <vector>
#include <queue>
using namespace std;

class CompareLastDigits {
public:
   bool operator()(int x, int y)
   {  return x % 10 > y % 10;
   }
};

int main()
{  priority_queue <int, vector<int>, CompareLastDigits>
      P;
   int x;
   P.push(123); P.push(51); P.push(1000); P.push(17);
   while (!P.empty())
   {  x = P.top();
      cout << "Retrieved element: " << x << endl;
      P.pop();
   }
   return 0;
}
```

In the output of this program, the inserted numbers 123, 51, 1000, 17 appear in ascending order of their last digits ($0 < 1 < 3 < 7$):

```
Retrieved element: 1000
Retrieved element: 51
Retrieved element: 123
Retrieved element: 17
```

Note that we really have to use a function object because the *priority_queue* template requires a type as its third argument. The identifier *CompareLastDigit* denotes such a type. The comparison

```
x % 10 > y % 10;
```

contains a greater-than character, which causes the element with the smallest last digit to be selected. This is similar to using *greater<int>* if the smallest element is to appear first.

6

Function Objects and Adaptors

6.1 Function Objects

Function objects, introduced in Sections 1.12 and 2.4, are sometimes considered confusing and mysterious. Let us experiment a little with this subject without using any STL facilities. The following program shows a class sq that we can use to compute the square x^2 of an integer x:

```
// funobj1.cpp: A simple function object.
#include <iostream.h>

struct sq {
    int operator()(int x)const {return x * x;}
};

int main()
{   cout << "5 * 5 = " << sq()(5) << endl; // 25
    return 0;
}
```

The keyword *struct* is frequently used instead of *class* if the class in question has only public members. Except for the default access rights (private for *class* and public for *struct*), these two keywords are equivalent.

Referring to Section 1.12, we know that the expression *sq*( ) calls the default constructor of class *sq*, so that this expression represents an object of that class. The line

```
int operator()(int x){return x * x;}
```

in this class defines the *operator*( ) in such a way that *sq*( )(5) is a valid function call, returning 25. It is important to distinguish the following expressions:

sq   a class (that is, a type), which we will call a *function class*
sq( )   a *function object*
sq( )(5)   a function call

Function objects offer all the possibilities of normal functions, but they offer some others besides, as the following program illustrates:

```
// funobj2.cpp: Function classes used as
//                 template arguments.
#include <iostream.h>

struct square {
    int operator()(int x)const {return x * x;}
};

struct cube {
    int operator()(int x)const {return x * x * x;}
};

template <class T>
class cont {
public:
    cont(int i): j(i){}
    void print()const {cout << T()(j) << endl;}
private:
    int j;
};

int main()
{   cont<square> numsq(10);
    numsq.print();  // Output: 100
    cont<cube> numcub(10);
    numcub.print(); // Output: 1000
    return 0;
}
```

In the *main* function of this program, function classes (*square* and *cube*) act as template arguments. We may regard *cont<T>* as a very restricted container, since it can store only one integer. However, it is very general in that the type parameter *T* can be any function class whose function takes an *int* argument and returns an *int* value. In this example, these function classes are *square* and *cube*. Although program *funobj2.cpp* seems to be very contrived, it may be helpful in understanding more interesting programs. For example, the *priority_queue* container also requires a function class as an argument, as we have seen at the end of the previous chapter.

The *operator*( ) functions in our above example have only one parameter, while there are two parameters in many other cases, such as with priority queues. Let us now use such functions with two parameters. We will use a template class *Pair-Select*, containing a print function that prints the smaller element of the pair according to a less-than relation of our own, supplied as a template argument. Let us also supply the type of the pair elements as template arguments. The following program uses two ordering relations. They are implemented as *binary predicates*, that is, as functions that have two parameters and return a logical value. Our first binary predicate, *LessThan*, is a template, so we can use it for any data type for which the operator < is defined. The second, *CompareLastDigits*, is a normal function class, not a template, almost identical to the one used in the last section of the previous chapter, but this one returns 1 if the final digit of the first argument is less than that of the second, and 0 otherwise.

```
// funobj3.cpp: The operator() function is a
//               binary predicate.
#include <iostream.h>

template <class T>
struct LessThan {
   bool operator()(const T &x, const T &y)const
   {  return x < y;
   }
};

struct CompareLastDigits {
   bool operator()(int x, int y)const
   {  return x % 10 < y % 10;
   }
};

template <class T, class Compare>
class PairSelect {
public:
   PairSelect(const T &x, const T &y): a(x), b(y){}
   void PrintSmaller()const
   {  cout << (Compare()(a, b) ? a : b) << endl;
   }
private:
   T a, b;
};
```

```
int main()
{ PairSelect<double, LessThan<double> > P(123.4, 98.7);
  P.PrintSmaller(); // Output: 98.7

  PairSelect<int, CompareLastDigits> Q(123, 98);
  Q.PrintSmaller(); // Output: 123
  return 0;
}
```

The program first displays the value 98.7 because this is less than the other *PairSelect* element, 123.4. Then it displays 123 because its last digit, 3, is less than the last digit of 98.

The STL template *less<T>* is very similar to the class template *LessThan<T>* of the program *funobj3.cpp*. You can find the following definition in the header *functional*:

```
template <class T>
struct less: binary_function<T, T, bool> {
   bool operator()(const T& x, const T& y) const
   { return x < y;
   }
};
```

The only difference between this STL class *less* and our class *LessThan* is that *less* is defined as a class derived from the base class *binary_function*. This class is empty but for some typedef declarations, and the same applies to its unary counter-part *unary_function*. The following definitions of these classes also occur in the header *functional*:

```
template <class Arg, class Result>
struct unary_function {
   typedef Arg argument_type;
   typedef Result result_type;
};

template <class Arg1, class Arg2, class Result>
struct binary_function {
   typedef Arg1 first_argument_type;
   typedef Arg2 second_argument_type;
   typedef Result result_type;
};
```

We do not require the typedef declarations of these two base classes for our present purpose, but they are in the header *functional* for the definition of binders and negators, to be discussed in a moment.

As you may expect, the program *funobj3.cpp* also works well if we replace our own *LessThan<T>* template class with the STL template class *less<T>*. To do this, you can modify this program as follows:

1. At the top of the program, add the two lines *#include <functional>* (or *#include <algorithm >*) and *using namespace std;*.
2. Remove the definition of the class *LessThan*.
3. Replace *LessThan* with *less* in the second line of the *main* function.

6.2 Unary Predicates and Binders

In mathematics, we can turn a function f of two arguments into one that has only one argument by keeping one argument of f constant. For example, we can define function g as

$$g(x) = f(x, c)$$

where c is a constant. Now suppose we want to use the STL template *less<T>* to count how may values of an *int* array a, of say, 10 elements, are less than 100. We have seen in Section 2.3 that there is a *count_if* algorithm for such tasks, but this requires a *unary predicate* rather than a binary one. This is very logical, since we have to deal with the condition

$$x < 100$$

in which only one variable occurs. This condition is obviously a special case of

$$x < y$$

We say that we want to *bind* the second argument of *less<T>* to the value 100. The way to do this in STL is by using a *binder*, which is a special case of a *function adaptor*. To turn a binary predicate into a unary one by binding its second argument, we use the binder *bind2nd*. In our example, the expression

```
bind2nd(less<int>(), 100)
```

is what we need to indicate that only the values less than 100 are to be counted. The following program illustrates this:

```
// binder.cpp: The bind2nd adaptor used to count
//     how many array elements are less than 100.
#include <iostream>
#include <algorithm>
#include <functional>
using namespace std;

int main()
{   int a[10] = {800, 3, 4, 600, 5, 6, 800, 71, 100, 2},
        n;   // (With BC5.2, count_if is different)
    n = count_if(a, a + 10, bind2nd(less<int>(), 100));
    cout << n << endl; // Output: 6
    return 0;
}
```

There is also a binder *bind1st* to bind the first argument. To demonstrate this, let us replace $x < 100$ with the equivalent condition

$$100 > x$$

We can obtain this by binding the first operand y of

$$y > x$$

to the value 100. The program *binder.cpp* will therefore give exactly the same result if we replace the call to *count_if* with this one:

```
n = count_if(a, a + 10, bind1st(greater<int>(), 100));
```

We will not discuss the definitions of *bind1st* and *bind2nd* in *functional*, since they are far more complicated than the way we use these binders in our programs.

6.3 Negators

Programmers frequently use the unary operator ! (not). For example, the expression

```
!(x < y)
```

is equivalent to

```
x >= y
```

The *not2* negator works in the same way for function objects that take two arguments. A negator is another kind of *function adaptor*; it is implemented as a template function that accepts a binary predicate object, such as *less<int>*( ), as an argument. We can therefore write

```
not2(less<int>())
```

instead of

```
greater_equal<int>
```

The following program demonstrates this. It sorts an array of five elements to place these in descending order:

```
// not2demo.cpp: The not2 adaptor demonstrated.
#include <iostream>
#include <algorithm>
#include <functional>
using namespace std;

int main()
{   int a[5] = {50, 30, 10, 40, 20};
    sort(a, a+5, not2(less<int>()));
    for (int i=0; i<5; i++) cout << a[i] << " ";
    // Output: 50 40 30 20 10
    cout << endl;
    return 0;
}
```

Instead of the above call to the sort algorithm, we could have written

```
sort(a, a+5, greater_equal<int>());
```

or simply

```
sort(a, a+5, greater<int>());
```

The function adaptor *not*1 takes a unary predicate object. Since the *bind1st* and *bind2nd* adaptors return a unary predicate, an expression such as

```
bind2nd(less<int>(), 100)
```

is a an acceptable argument for *not*1, as this program shows:

```
// not1demo.cpp: The not1 adaptor demonstrated.
#include <iostream>
#include <algorithm>
#include <functional>
using namespace std;

int main()
{   int a[10] = {800, 3, 4, 600, 5, 6, 800, 71, 100, 2},
        n;
    // Count how many elements are not less than 100:
    n = count_if(a, a + 10,
        not1(bind2nd(less<int>(), 100)));
    cout << n << endl; // Output: 4
    return 0;
}
```

Note that counting how many elements of the array are at least 100 could have been done by the following, simpler call to *count_if*:

```
n = count_if(a, a + 10,
    bind2nd(greater_equal<int>(), 100));
```

In either case, the output is 4, since exactly four elements (800, 600, 800, 100) of array *a* are not less than 100.

6.4 Two Useful STL Base Classes

You may wonder if we could not have used a simpler example than

```
sort(a, a+5, not2(less<int>()));
```

(occurring in program *not2demo.cpp* in the previous section) to discuss the use of *not2*. In particular, it would be interesting if we could apply *not2* to a function object of our own, writing, for example,

```
sort(a, a+5, not2(iLessThan()));
```

where *iLessThan* is a function class defined as

```
struct iLessThan {                      // ???
bool operator()(int x, int y)const {return x < y;}
};
```

However, that would not compile. The *not2* adaptor requires that its argument type is a class derived from the template *binary_function*, introduced in Section 6.1. This is very easy to realize by inserting

```
: binary_function<int, int, bool>
```

immediately after the name *iLessThan* in the first of the above three program lines. The three template arguments *int*, *int* and *bool* denote the types of the two arguments and of the result, which we would use if we wrote a simple function, such as

```
bool lessthan(int x, int y){return x < y;}
```

for the same purpose.

Using *binary_function<int, int, bool>* as a base class of class *iLessThan*, we obtain the following complete program, which is equivalent to *not2demo.cpp* of the previous section:

```
// not2own.cpp: The not2 adaptor applied to a function
//                object of our own.
#include <iostream>
#include <algorithm>
#include <functional>
using namespace std;

struct iLessThan: binary_function<int, int, bool> {
bool operator()(int x, int y)const {return x < y;}
};

int main()
{   int a[5] = {50, 30, 10, 40, 20};
    sort(a, a+5, not2(iLessThan()));
    for (int i=0; i<5; i++) cout << a[i] << " ";
    // Output: 50 40 30 20 10
    cout << endl;
    return 0;
}
```

We can also apply the *not*1 adaptor to a function object of our own. In program *not1demo.cpp* of the previous section we used *not*1 in the expression

```
not1(bind2nd(less<int>(), 100))
```

to count how many elements of an array were not less than 100. In this expression, we will replace

```
bind2nd(less<int>(), 100)
```

with the simpler form

```
LessThan100()
```

where *LessThan*100 is a class of our own, as the following complete program shows:

```
// not1own.cpp: The not1 adaptor applied to a
//                function object of our own.
#include <iostream>
#include <algorithm>
#include <functional>
using namespace std;

struct LessThan100: unary_function<int, bool> {
bool operator()(int x)const {return x < 100;}
};
```

```
int main()
{   int a[10] = {800, 3, 4, 600, 5, 6, 800, 71, 100, 2},
        n;
    // Count how many elements are not less than 100:
    n = count_if(a, a+10, not1(LessThan100()));
    cout << n << endl; // Output: 4
    return 0;
}
```

In this case the part

```
: unary_function<int, bool>
```

indicates the base class from which the class *LessThan*100 is derived. We write
unary_function<int, bool> because *not*1 takes a unary predicate object with a single
int argument and returning a *bool* value. Recall that we have already seen the
definition of this *unary_function* class in Section 6.1.

6.5 Function Objects and *transform*

As we have seen in Section 2.4, STL provides the following template classes, which
we can use as function objects by adding a pair of parentheses:

```
plus<T>            minus<T>
multiplies<T>      divides<T>         modulus<T>
equal_to<T>        not_equal_to<T>
greater<T>         less<T>
greater_equal<T>   less_equal<T>
logical_and<T>     logical_or<T>
negate<T>          logical_not<T>
```

To illustrate some of those we have not yet used, let us first introduce the *transform*
algorithms. There are two: one for unary and one for binary operations. We use
them to transform all elements of a range. For example, suppose that we want to
use the elements $a[i]$ of an *int* array a to assign values $b[i] = -a[i]$ to another array,
b. One way to achieve this is by a call to the *transform* algorithm for unary
operations, using the *negate<T>* template, as the following program shows:

```
// negate.cpp: The transform algorithm and negate<T>.
#include <iostream>
#include <algorithm>
#include <functional>
using namespace std;

int main()
{   int a[5] = {10, 20, -18, 40, 50}, b[5];
    transform(a, a + 5, b, negate<int>());
```

```
      for (int i=0; i<5; i++) cout << b[i] << "   ";
      // Output: -10  -20   18  -40  -50
      cout << endl;
      return 0;
   }
```

The function object *logical_not<T>*( ) is very similar to *negate<T>*( ). If we write

```
   transform(a, a + 5, b, logical_not<int>());
```

then the array *b* will be assigned the values $b[i] = !\, a[i]$. In other words, each element *b[i]* will be 0 if *a[i]* is nonzero and it will be 1 if *a[i]* is zero. Recall that we may write *bool*, *true* and *false* instead of *int*, 1 and 0. Instead of both a source array *a* and a destination array *b*, we may use only one. For example, the call

```
   transform(a, a + 5, a, negate<int>());
```

has the effect of multiplying the five elements of array *a* by –1.

So much for the unary version of *transform*. There is also a version that uses two source arrays instead of one and accepts a binary function object. Suppose, for example, that we want to use the arrays *a* and *b* to compute the sum array *s*, where

$$s[i] = a[i] + b[i]$$

The following program shows the use of the *plus<int>* template to achieve this:

```
   // plus.cpp: The transform algorithm and plus<T>.
   #include <iostream>
   #include <algorithm>
   #include <functional>
   using namespace std;

   int main()
   {  int a[5] = {10, 20, -18, 40, 50},
          b[5] = { 2,  2,   5,  3,  1}, s[5];
      transform(a, a + 5, b, s, plus<int>());
      for (int i=0; i<5; i++) cout << s[i] << "   ";
       // Output: 12   22  -13   43   51
      cout << endl;
      return 0;
   }
```

Instead of a separate array *s*, we can use one of the source arrays *a* and *b* if we like, replacing *s* with either *a* or *b* in the call to *transform*.

Instead of *plus*, corresponding to +, we can use one of the other arithmetic binary function objects: *minus*, *multiplies*, *divides* and *modulus*, for –, *, / and %, respectively. This also applies to the binary function objects *equal_to*, *not_equal_to*, *greater*, *less*, *greater_equal*, *less_equal*, *logical_and* and *logical_or*, corresponding to the operators ==, !=, >, <, >=, <=, && and ||, but these return a *bool* value, and the last two of them (*logical_and* and *logical_or*) are normally applied to arguments that are also of type *bool*. Although this list seems impressive, it will often lack some special operation that we want to use in connection with the *transform*. In such cases we can use function objects of our own, defining a class derived from either the *binary_function* or the *unary_function* templates, as discussed in the previous section. For example, suppose that we are again given the two *int* arrays *a* and *b* and that we want to compute the array *result* as follows:

```
result[i] = a[i] + 2 * b[i]
```

(for, say, *i* = 0, 1, ..., 5). The following program shows how a class *compute*, written for this purpose, can be used:

```cpp
// compute.cpp: The transform algorithm and a
//              function object of our own.
#include <iostream>
#include <algorithm>
#include <functional>
using namespace std;

struct compute: binary_function<int, int, int> {
    int operator()(int x, int y)const{return x + 2 * y;}
};

int main()
{   int a[5] = {10, 20, -18, 40, 50},
        b[5] = { 2,  2,   5,  3,   1}, result[5];
    transform(a, a + 5, b, result, compute());
    for (int i=0; i<5; i++) cout << result[i] << "   ";
        // Output: 14   24   -8   46   52
    cout << endl;
    return 0;
}
```

The same applies to the *transform* version that takes a unary function object. For example, if we want to replace all five elements *a[i]* of the *int* array *a* with the value 1.0/(*a[i]* * *a[i]* + 1) (using array *a* as both a source and a destination), we can do this by using a class derived from the *unary_function* template, as the following program shows:

```cpp
// compute1.cpp: Replacing a[i] with 1.0/(a[i]*a[i]+1).
#include <iostream>
#include <algorithm>
#include <functional>
using namespace std;

struct compute1: unary_function<int, double> {
    double operator()(int x)const{return 1.0/(x*x + 1);}
};
```

```
int main()
{   int a[5] = {2, 0, 1, 3, 7};
    double b[5];
    transform(a, a + 5, b, compute1());
    for (int i=0; i<5; i++) cout << b[i] << " ";
    // Output: 0.2 1 0.5 0.1 0.02
    cout << endl;
    return 0;
}
```

6.6 Iterator Adaptors

There are two kinds of iterator adaptors: insert iterators and reverse iterators. In this section, we will encounter some iterator types that we have already discussed and some new ones besides.

Insert iterators

As we have seen in program *copy2.cpp* in Section 1.6, algorithms such as *copy* will copy in insert mode, if we write, for example,

```
copy(v.begin(), v.end(), inserter(L, i));
```

This insert iterator *inserter* is very general in that we supply the position, *i* in this example, where insertion is to take place. If insertion (in the container *L*) is to take place at the end, we can write *L.end*( ), as this program shows:

```
// copy3.cpp: Copying a vector using 'inserter'.

#include <iostream>
#include <vector>
#include <list>
using namespace std;

int main()
{   int a[4] = {10, 20, 30, 40};
    vector<int> v(a, a+4);
    list<int> L(2, 123);
    copy(v.begin(), v.end(), inserter(L, L.end()));
    list<int>::iterator i;
    for (i=L.begin(); i != L.end(); ++i)
       cout << *i << " "; // Output: 123 123 10 20 30 40
    cout << endl;
    return 0;
}
```

Since inserting at the end is a very common operation, there is a special insert iterator for it, called *back_inserter*. The above program works in exactly the same way if we replace the call to the *copy* algorithm with this one:

```
copy(v.begin(), v.end(), back_inserter(L));
```

Since *back_inserter* always inserts at the back, it takes only one argument, the container.

Yet another insert iterator, *front_inserter*, works in a peculiar way: every newly inserted element is placed at the front, which has the effect that the values will occur in reverse order. For example, if we replace the call to the *copy* algorithm in program *copy3.cpp* with the line

```
copy(v.begin(), v.end(), front_inserter(L));
```

then the program will produce the following output:

```
40 30 20 10 123 123
```

So far, we have been using insert iterators only as arguments of algorithms, such as *copy* and *merge*. We can also use them in other ways. For example, instead of

```
L.push_front(111); L.push_back(999);
```

we can write

```
*front_inserter(L) = 111; *back_inserter(L) = 999;
```

Reverse iterators

As we have seen in Section 3.1, we have the following iterators for type *vector<int>*, and it goes without saying that there are similar iterators for other types, such as *list<double>*.

```
vector<int>::iterator
vector<int>::reverse_iterator
vector<int>::const_iterator
vector<int>::const_reverse_iterator
```

Recall that in Section 1.2 we have used a reverse iterator in the following fragment to display all elements of vector *v* in reverse order.

```
vector<int>::reverse_iterator i;
for (i=v.rbegin(); i != v.rend(); ++i)
    cout << *i << " ";
```

The *const* versions are required if the container itself has the *const* attribute, as is the case in the following program, in which the function *showlist* is a modified version of the one discussed in Section 1.3:

```
// c_iter.cpp: const_iterator and
//             const_reverse_iterator.
#include <iostream>
#include <list>
using namespace std;

void showlist(const list<int> &x)
{  // Forward:
   list<int>::const_iterator i;
   for (i=x.begin(); i != x.end(); ++i)
      cout << *i << " ";
   cout << endl;    //  Output: 10 20 30
   // Backward:
   list<int>::const_reverse_iterator j;
   for (j=x.rbegin(); j != x.rend(); ++j)
      cout << *j << " ";
   cout << endl;    //  Output: 30 20 10
}

int main()
{  list<int> L;
   L.push_back(10); L.push_back(20); L.push_back(30);
   showlist(L);
   return 0;
}
```

We cannot omit the two occurrences of *const_* in the function *showlist*, unless we also omit the word *const* in the first line of this function. Since this function does not alter the list in question, it is considered good programming practice to maintain this occurrence of *const*.

Stream iterators

We have used stream iterators in Section 1.9 and elsewhere in connection with the *copy* algorithm. It is also possible to use these iterators in a more elementary way, and the second argument taken by an *ostream_iterator* constructor need not be a string consisting only of a space, as the following program shows:

```
// outiter.cpp: Output iterator; assignment statements
//              reading data from a file.
#include <iostream>
#include <vector>
#include <iterator>
using namespace std;
```

```
int main()
{   ostream_iterator<int> i(cout, "abc\n");
    *i++ = 123;
    *i++ = 456;
    cout << endl;
    return 0;
}
```

This program produces the following output:

```
123abc
456abc
```

Since the *ostream_iterator* template is the only STL aspect of this program, the program works if we write *#include <iterator>* instead of *#include <vector>*.

Things are always a little bit trickier with input, because we want to be able to detect the end of the input stream. Recall that we have discussed this end-of-file subject in Section 1.9. The following is a very strange solution to the problem of reading all integers from the file *num.txt*, where this is a text file containing only integers in the usual format:

```
// initer.cpp: Input iterator; assignment statements
//              performing input from a file.
#include <iostream>
#include <fstream>
#include <vector>
#include <iterator>
using namespace std;

int main()
{   ifstream file("num.txt");
    if (file)
    {   istream_iterator<int> i(file), eof;
        int x;
        while (i != eof)
        {   x = *i++;
            cout << x << " ";
        }
    } else cout << "Cannot open file num.txt.";
    cout << endl;
    return 0;
}
```

For example, if the file *num.txt* consists of the two lines

```
10 20
30
```

the program will produce the following output:

```
10 20 30
```

7

Generic Algorithms

This chapter gives an overview of all STL algorithms, also known as generic algorithms. We will refer to previous discussions about algorithms that we already know, and deal with new ones in more detail. There are four categories, which we will discuss in this order:

- Nonmutating sequence algorithms
- Mutating sequence algorithms
- Sorting-related algorithms
- Generalized numeric algorithms

Although STL algorithms are templates, we normally think of them as *functions* because of the way they are used. We will often use arrays of integers as examples of sequence containers. Instead, we can use other containers, depending on the iterator categories of their arguments. For example, since the *sort* algorithm takes random-access arguments, we cannot apply it to a *list* container, as discussed in Section 1.3. We will therefore start each section of this chapter with an overview of the algorithms that are discussed in it, indicating the iterator types of the arguments. We will do this in the form of prototypes (or template declarations), omitting the *template<...>* part and placing the algorithm names in italic at the end of a line so you can easily find them.

You may at first find these lists of prototypes rather tedious because of their similarity and because many long type names (which are template parameters), such as *RandomAcessIterator*, occur in them. However, once you are somewhat familiar with the algorithms in question, these prototypes will enable you to obtain useful information very quickly. For example, consider the parameters of *sort*, written in the prototype as *RandomAcessIterator first, RandomAcessIterator last*. Since a list does not provide a random-access iterator, it is clear from this prototype that we cannot use the *sort* algorithm for lists. It may be helpful to read Section 1.9 once again to understand the meaning of the iterator parameter types. In particular you should remember the iterator hierarchy. The higher the iterator level of a parameter, the more limited the function's use will be. The high-level random-access iterators allow operations such as $i + n$, which prevents us from applying them to lists.

7.1 Nonmutating Sequence Algorithms

The algorithms discussed in this section only *inspect* sequences, without modifying them.

7.1.1 The *find, count, for_each, find_first_of* and *find_end* Algorithms

As the references in comments indicate, we have already discussed most of the following algorithms:

```
InputIterator find        // Discussed in Section 1.5
   (InputIterator first,  InputIterator last,
    const T& value);
InputIterator find_if     // Discussed in Section 1.13
   (InputIterator first,  InputIterator last,
    Predicate pred);
void for_each             // Discussed in Section 2.2
   (InputIterator first,  InputIterator last,
    Function f);
difference_type count     // Discussed in Section 2.3
   (InputIterator first,  InputIterator last,
    const T& value);
difference_type count_if // Discussed in Section 2.3
   (InputIterator first, InputIterator last,
    Predicate pred);
ForwardIterator1 find_first_of
   (ForwardIterator1 first1, ForwardIterator1 last1,
    ForwardIterator2 first2, ForwardIterator2 last2);
ForwardIterator1 find_first_of
   (ForwardIterator1 first1,ForwardIterator1 last1,
    ForwardIterator2 first2,ForwardIterator2 last2,
    BinaryPredicate pred);
ForwardIterator1 find_end
   (ForwardIterator1 first1, ForwardIterator1 last1,
    ForwardIterator2 first2, ForwardIterator2 last2);
```

```
ForwardIterator1 find_end
   (ForwardIterator1 first1, ForwardIterator1 last1,
    ForwardIterator2 first2, ForwardIterator2 last2,
    BinaryPredicate pred);
```

We will not repeat our previous discussion of *find*, *find_if*, *for_each*, *count*, and *count_if*.

The algorithm *find_first_of* is similar to *find*, but instead of looking for an element that is equal to a given value, it looks for an element of the first range that is equal to some element of the second. If there are such elements in the first range, it returns the position of the first of them. By contrast, *find_end* returns the start position of the last occurrence of the entire second sequence in the first. (If you prefer the start position of the *first* occurrence, use *search*, to be discussed in Section 7.1.5). If no match is found, *find_first_of* and *find_end* return *last*1. The following program demonstrates both algorithms:

```cpp
// find_end: The find_first_of and find_end algorithms.
#include <iostream>
#include <algorithm>
using namespace std;

int main()
{   int a[10] = {3, 2, 5, 7, 5, 8, 7, 5, 8, 5},
        b[2] = {5, 8}, *p1, *p2;
    p1 = find_first_of(a, a+10, b, b+2);
    p2 = find_end(a, a+10, b, b+2);
    cout << p1 - a << " " << p2 - a << endl;
    return 0;
}
```

The output of this program is:

```
2  7
```

since $a[2]$ (= 5) is the first element of a that also occurs in b and $a[7]$ (= 5) is the last start element of the entire sequence 5, 8 (as given by b) occurring in a.

There are also versions of *find_first_of* and *find_end* that takes an extra argument for comparisons, a binary predicate. We can use this predicate to replace the test for equality with a different one, as we will discuss in detail for the next algorithm, *adjacent_find*.

7.1.2 Adjacent Find

```
ForwardIterator adjacent_find
   (ForwardIterator first, ForwardIterator last);
ForwardIterator adjacent_find
   (ForwardIterator first, ForwardIterator last,
    BinaryPredicate binary_pred);
```

There are two algorithms *adjacent_find* to search a sequence container. The first looks for adjacent elements $a[k]$ and $a[k+1]$ that are equal; the second for adjacent elements that satisfy some specified condition. The following program demonstrates both versions. It searches the array *a* four times:

1. for two elements $a[k]$ and $a[k+1]$ elements that are equal;
2. for two elements $a[k]$ and $a[k+1]$ elements satisfying $a[k] > a[k+1]$;
3. for two elements $a[k]$ and $a[k+1]$ elements satisfying $a[k]^2 = a[k+1]$;
4. for two elements $a[k]$ and $a[k+1]$ elements satisfying $a[k]^3 = a[k+1]$.

If the adjacent elements searched for are not found, the *adjacent_find* function returns the iterator value just after the final element, as is usual; for example, if we had used a vector *v* instead of an array *a*, that iterator value would have been equal to *v.end*( ). The values of array *a* are such that the first three search operations succeed, while the fourth fails:

```
// adjacent.cpp: The adjacent_find algorithms.
#include <iostream>
#include <iomanip>
#include <algorithm>
#include <functional>
using namespace std;

bool is_square(int x, int y){return x * x == y;}
bool is_cube(int x, int y){return x * x * x == y;}

int main()
{   int a[10] =
    {5, 10, 28, 20, 10, 5, 25, 10, 10, 90}, *p, k;
    for (k=0; k<10; k++) cout << setw(3) << k;
    cout << endl;
    for (k=0; k<10; k++) cout << setw(3) << a[k];
    cout << endl;
    p = adjacent_find(a, a+10);
    k = p - a;
    if (k != 10)
       cout << "a[k] = a[k+1], found at k = " << k
            << endl;
    p = adjacent_find(a, a+10, greater<int>());
    k = p - a;
    if (k != 10)
       cout << "a[k] > a[k+1], found at k = " << k
            << endl;
    p = adjacent_find(a, a+10, is_square);
    k = p - a;
    if (k != 10)
       cout << "a[k]*a[k] == a[k+1], found at k = "
            << k << endl;
```

```
    p = adjacent_find(a, a+10, is_cube);
    k = p - a;
    if (k != 10)
        cout << "a[k]*a[k]*a[k] == a[k+1], found at k = "
            << k << endl;
    else cout << "If not found: k = " << k << endl;
    return 0;
}
```

This program produces the following output:

```
  0  1  2  3  4  5  6  7  8  9
  5 10 28 20 10  5 25 10 10 90
a[k] = a[k+1], found at k = 7
a[k] > a[k+1], found at k = 2
a[k]*a[k] == a[k+1], found at k = 5
If not found: k = 10
```

The predicates in this program are written as functions. As you will remember from Chapter 6 and elsewhere, we could instead have used function objects. For example, we can replace the function *is_square* with this class definition:

```
struct sq {
bool operator()(int x, int y){return x * x == y;}
};
```

provided we also replace

```
    p = adjacent_find(a, a+10, is_square);
```

with

```
    p = adjacent_find(a, a+10, sq());
```

This principle also applies to other uses of predicates in this chapter.

7.1.3 Mismatch

```
pair<InputIterator1, InputIterator2> mismatch
    (InputIterator1 first1, InputIterator1 last1,
     InputIterator2 first2);
pair<InputIterator1, InputIterator2> mismatch
    (InputIterator1 first1, InputIterator1 last1,
     InputIterator2 first2, BinaryPredicate binary_pred);
```

There are two versions of the *mismatch* algorithm. The first searches two parallel sequence containers for two elements in the same position that are unequal. In other words, if we denote these elements by x and y, we have $!(x == y)$. The second version takes a predicate as an additional argument, which is used instead of the equality operator $==$. The following program demonstrates both:

```
// mismatch.cpp: The mismatch algorithms.

#include <iostream>
#include <iomanip>
#include <algorithm>

using namespace std;

bool smalldif(int a, int b){return abs(a - b) < 25;}

int main()
{   int a[4] = {50, 80, 30, 90},
        b[5] = {50, 80, 10, 40, 20}, *pa, *pb, k;
    pair<int*, int*> difpos(0, 0);
    for (k=0; k<5; k++) cout << setw(3) << k;
    cout << endl;
    for (k=0; k<4; k++) cout << setw(3) << a[k];
    cout << endl;
    for (k=0; k<5; k++) cout << setw(3) << b[k];
    cout << endl;
    difpos = mismatch(a, a+4, b);
    pa = difpos.first;
    pb = difpos.second;
    cout << "Different elements "
         << *pa << " and " << *pb
         << " found at position " << pa - a << endl;
    difpos = mismatch(a, a+4, b, smalldif);
    pa = difpos.first;
    pb = difpos.second;
    cout << "Difference of at least 25 found between\n"
         << *pa << " and " << *pb
         << " at position " << pa - a << endl;

    return 0;
}
```

In both cases, mismatched elements are found, as the following output demonstrates:

```
  0  1  2  3  4
 50 80 30 90
 50 80 10 40 20
Different elements 30 and 10 found at position 2
Difference of at least 25 found between
90 and 40 at position 3
```

Note that the second sequence must be at least as long as the first. If no mismatched elements had been found (which would be the case if we replaced 25 with 250), the returned pair of iterator values would have corresponded with position 4 of the arrays.

7.1.4 Equal

```
bool equal
    (InputIterator1 first1, InputIterator1 last1,
     InputIterator2 first2);
bool equal
    (InputIterator1 first1, InputIterator1 last1,
     InputIterator2 first2, BinaryPredicate binary_pred);
```

There are also two *equal* algorithms. The first determines whether two sequences (as far as they are compared) are equal; the second works similarly but takes a predicate as an argument, which is used instead of the equality operator = =. The following program demonstrates both versions:

```
// equal.cpp: The equal algorithms.

#include <iostream>
#include <iomanip>
#include <algorithm>

using namespace std;

bool approx(int a, int b){return abs(a - b) <= 1;}

int main()
{   int a[4] = {50, 80, 30, 90},
        b[5] = {50, 80, 30, 90, 20},
        c[4] = {50, 79, 30, 90};
    cout << equal(a, a+4, b) << endl;          // 1
    cout << equal(a, a+4, c) << endl;          // 0
    cout << equal(a, a+4, c, approx) << endl; // 1
    return 0;
}
```

The function equal returns a *bool* value *true* (= 1) or *false* (= 0), as the comments indicate. Since the four elements of *a* are equal to the first four elements of *b*, the first call to *equal* returns *true*. The second call returns *false* because $a[1] = 80$ and $c[1] = 79$. In the third call the difference $80 - 79$ is small enough (with regard to the predicate *approx*) to make the function *equal* return *true*. Note that the function *equal* does not return any information about the position of a mismatch, if any. If such information is desired, the *mismatch* algorithm should be used instead.

7.1.5 Search

```
ForwardIterator1 search
    (ForwardIterator1 first1, ForwardIterator1 last1,
     ForwardIterator2 first2, ForwardIterator2 last2);
ForwardIterator1 search
    (ForwardIterator1 first1, ForwardIterator1 last1,
     ForwardIterator2 first2, ForwardIterator2 last2,
     BinaryPredicate binary_pred);
```

The first version of the *search* algorithm is a generalization of the well-known C string-searching function *strstr*, as used in this example:

```
#include <string.h>
...
char *p = strstr("ABCDEF", "CD"); /* *p == 'C' */
```

The *strstr* library function returns *NULL* if the second argument is not a substring of the first.

The first version of *search*, used to search a (larger) array for a (smaller) subarray, takes two arguments for the larger array and two for the smaller. The second version takes a fifth argument, which is a predicate that is used instead of the equality operator ==. The following program demonstrates both *search* algorithms:

```
// search.cpp: The search algorithms.
#include <iostream>
#include <algorithm>
using namespace std;

bool dif1(int x, int y){return x + 1 == y;}

int main()
{   int a[6] = {10, 20, 50, 30, 60, 40},
        b[2] = {50, 30},
        c[3] = {51, 31, 61}, *p1, *p2, *p3;
    p1 = search(a, a+6, b, b+2); cout << p1 - a << " ";
    p2 = search(a, a+6, c, c+3); cout << p2 - a << " ";
    p3 = search(a, a+6, c, c+3, dif1); cout << p3 - a
       << endl; // Output: 2 6 2
    return 0;
}
```

In the first call, the elements $b[0]$ and $b[1]$ are found as $a[2]$ and $a[3]$, so that *search* returns the address of $a[2]$, which is placed in $p1$. Since the three values stored in array c are not found in array a, the pointer $p2$ is given a value so that it points to the element just after the final one of array a. Finally, the address of $a[2]$ is placed in $p3$ because the elements 50, 30 and 60 of array a correspond with 51, 31 and 61 of array c according to the *dif*1 predicate.

7.2 Mutating Sequence Algorithms

The algorithms of this section modify the sequence they operate upon.

7.2.1 Transform

```
OutputIterator transform
    (InputIterator first, InputIterator last,
     OutputIterator result, UnaryOperation unary_op);
OutputIterator transform
    (InputIterator1 first1, InputIterator1 last1,
     InputIterator2 first2, OutputIterator result,
     BinaryOperation binary_op);
```

We have discussed the *transform* algorithms in Section 6.5, when we were dealing with function objects. Recall that there are two different transform algorithms: one is based on only one sequence and the other on two. The following program uses both algorithms in a way different from Section 6.5 in that we are now using normal functions (not function objects) as arguments. Since the vector *result* is initially empty, the first call to *transform* works in insert mode (by using *inserter*), as discussed in Section 1.6. After this, *result* consists of five elements so we can use overwrite mode in the second call to overwrite these elements:

```
// transfor.cpp: Two transform algorithms.
#include <iostream>
#include <vector>
#include <algorithm>
using namespace std;

int plus1(int x){return x + 1;}
int largersq(int x, int y){return x > y ? x*x : y*y;}

int main()
{   int a[5] = {2, -4, 3, 5, 1},
        b[5] = {1, -3, 5, 2, 4};
    vector<int> result;
    transform(a, a + 5,
        inserter(result, result.begin()), plus1);
    copy(result.begin(), result.end(),
        ostream_iterator<int>(cout, " "));
    cout << endl;  // Output: 3 -3 4 6 2
    transform(a, a+5, b, result.begin(), largersq);
    copy(result.begin(), result.end(),
        ostream_iterator<int>(cout, " "));
    cout << endl;  // Output: 4 9 25 25 16
    return 0;
}
```

As the comments indicate, the first result is obtained by adding 1 to all elements of array *a*. The second call to *transform* computes the squares of the larger of corresponding elements of *a* and *b*. For example, we have *result*[0] = 4, since this is the square of the larger element (2) of *a*[0] and *b*[0].

7.2.2 Copy

```
OutputIterator copy
   (InputIterator first1, InputIterator last1,
    OutputIterator first2);
OutputIterator copy_backward
   (BidirectionalIterator first1,
    BidirectionalIterator last1,
    BidirectionalIterator last2);
```

We have discussed the *copy* algorithm in Section 1.6. In that section, the source and the destination of the copying process did not overlap. If they do, we must carefully choose between the algorithms *copy*, which proceeds forward, and *copy_backward*. For example, if we want to move the elements *a*[1], *a*[2] and *a*[3] of an array *a* one position to the left, an elementary way of doing is as follows:

```
for (i=1; i<4; i++) a[i-1] = a[i];
```

The *copy* algorithm can do this in the same way, as the following program demonstrates:

```
// copy1.cpp: Shifting array elements to the left.

#include <iostream>
#include <algorithm>
using namespace std;

int main()
{   int a[4] = {10, 20, 30, 40}, i;
    cout << "Before shifting left: ";
    for (i=0; i<4; i++) cout << a[i] << " " ;
    copy(a+1, a+4, a);
    cout << "\nAfter shifting left:  ";
    for (i=0; i<4; i++) cout << a[i] << " " ;
    cout << endl;
    return 0;
}
```

Recall that the first two arguments of *copy* specify the source and the third the destination. This program shifts three array elements one position to the left, as its output shows:

```
Before shifting left: 10 20 30 40
After shifting left:  20 30 40 40
```

The opposite operation, shifting the array elements $a[0]$, $a[1]$ and $a[2]$ of a four-element array one position to the right, could be written as follows:

```
for (i=2; i>=0; i--) a[i+1] = a[i];
```

Note that we should go backward in this case, decrementing i. The following program shows how the *copy_backward* algorithm can perform the same task:

```
// copy2.cpp: Shifting array elements to the right.

#include <iostream>
#include <algorithm>
using namespace std;

int main()
{   int a[4] = {10, 20, 30, 40}, i;
    cout << "Before shifting right: ";
    for (i=0; i<4; i++) cout << a[i] << " " ;
    copy_backward(a, a+3, a+4);
    cout << "\nAfter shifting right:   ";
    for (i=0; i<4; i++) cout << a[i] << " " ;
    cout << endl;
    return 0;
}
```

As with *copy*, the first two arguments of *copy_backward* specify the source. However, the third argument indicates the 'past-the-end' position of the destination; in other words, this value will be decremented *before* each step, including the first one. The output of this program is as follows:

```
Before shifting right: 10 20 30 40
After shifting right:  10 10 20 30
```

The above program contains several occurrences of the following line:

```
for (i=0; i<4; i++) cout << a[i] << " " ;
```

In each case we could instead have used the *copy* algorithm in the following way, as we have discussed in Section 1.9:

```
copy(a, a+4, ostream_iterator<int>(cout, " "));
```

We will use this method in some of the programs that follow.

7.2.3 Rotate

```
void rotate
    (ForwardIterator first, ForwardIterator middle,
     ForwardIterator last);
void rotate_copy
    (ForwardIterator first, ForwardIterator middle,
     ForwardIterator last, OutputIterator result);
```

Instead of shifting some positions to the left or to the right, we sometimes want to rotate all elements of a sequence container (such as an array). For example, starting with

```
10 20 30 40
```

we may want to obtain the following sequence;

```
20 30 40 10
```

This will normally be regarded as 'rotate left by one position'. However, we can also view it as a 'rotate-right by three positions'. There is therefore only one *rotate* algorithm. Instead of specifying the number of positions and choosing between left and right, we simply indicate which element is to appear at the front. The argument used for this purpose is the second, the first and the third specifying the range in question. The above rotation, when applied to an array a of four elements, therefore requires the following call:

```
rotate(a, a+1, a+4);
```

The argument $a + 1$ indicates that the old element $a[1] = 20$ is to appear as the new initial element $a[0]$. Here is a complete demonstration program:

```
// rotate.cpp: Rotations.
#include <iostream>
#include <algorithm>
using namespace std;

int main()
{   int a[4] = {10, 20, 30, 40};
    cout << "Initial contents of array a: ";
    copy(a, a+4, ostream_iterator<int>(cout, " "));
    rotate(a, a+1, a+4);
    cout << "\nAfter rotate(a, a+1, a+4):    ";
    copy(a, a+4, ostream_iterator<int>(cout, " "));
    cout << endl;
    return 0;
}
```

This program produces the following output:

```
Initial contents of array a: 10 20 30 40
After rotate(a, a+1, a+4):    20 30 40 10
```

If the call to *rotate* in this program was followed by

```
rotate(a, a+3, a+4);
```

we would specify that the element $a[3] = 10$ is to become $a[0]$ again, which would result in the original array contents 10, 20, 30, 40 again.

There is also the *rotate_copy* function, which places the result in a copy of the original container, so that the latter one is not changed. The container in which the result is to appear is given as a fourth argument, as the following program shows:

```
// rotcopy.cpp: The rotate_copy algorithm.

#include <iostream>
#include <algorithm>
using namespace std;

int main()
{  int a[4] = {10, 20, 30, 40}, b[4];
   rotate_copy(a, a+1, a+4, b);
   copy(b, b+4, ostream_iterator<int>(cout, " "));
   cout << endl; // Output: 20 30 40 10
   return 0;
}
```

7.2.4 Swap

```
void swap
   (T& x, T& y);
void iter_swap
   (ForwardIterator1 a, ForwardIterator b);
ForwardIterator swap_ranges
   (ForwardIterator1 first1, ForwardIterator1 last1,
    ForwardIterator2 first2);
```

The *swap* algorithm simply swaps the values of two objects of the same type, as this program shows:

```
// swap.cpp: Swap.

#include <iostream>
#include <algorithm>
using namespace std;
```

```
int main()
{   double a = 3.14159,
            b = 2.71828;
    swap(a, b);
    cout << a << " " << b << endl;
    //   2.71828      3.14159
    return 0;
}
```

If we are given two iterator values, we can use the *iter_swap* algorithm to swap the values referred to by these iterators, as the following program illustrates:

```
// it_swap.cpp: The iter_swap algorithm.

#include <iostream>
#include <list>
#include <algorithm>
using namespace std;

int main()
{   list<int> L;
    list<int>::iterator i, j;
    L.push_back(123);
    L.push_back(456);
    copy(L.begin(), L.end(),
        ostream_iterator<int>(cout, " "));
    cout << endl;   // Output: 123 456
    i = L.begin();
    j = i;
    ++j;
    iter_swap(i, j);
    copy(L.begin(), L.end(),
        ostream_iterator<int>(cout, " "));
    cout << endl;   // Output: 456 123
    return 0;
}
```

The *swap_ranges* algorithm exchanges two ranges of values. These containers must not overlap, and they may be different types of container, as the following program illustrates:

```
// swranges.cpp: Swap ranges.

#include <iostream>
#include <vector>
#include <algorithm>

using namespace std;
```

```
int main()
{   int a[3] = {10, 20, 30};
    vector<int> v;
    v.push_back(100); v.push_back(200); v.push_back(300);
    swap_ranges(v.begin(), v.end(), a);
    cout << "After swap_ranges:\n";
    cout << "i    a[i]    v[i]\n";
    for (int i=0; i<3; i++)
       cout << i << "    " << a[i] << "        "
            << v[i] << endl;
    return 0;
}
```

This program produces the following output:

```
After swap_ranges:
i    a[i]    v[i]
0    100     10
1    200     20
2    300     30
```

As the above program illustrates, the first two arguments of *swap_ranges* specify one range and the third argument indicates the beginning of the other. Since the swap operation is symmetric in its two operands, the program also works correctly if we replace the call

```
swap_ranges(v.begin(), v.end(), a);
```

with the following one:

```
swap_ranges(a, a+3, v.begin());
```

7.2.5 Replace

```
void replace
    (ForwardIterator first, ForwardIterator last,
     const T& old_value, const T& new_value);
void replace_if
    (ForwardIterator first, ForwardIterator last,
     Predicate pred, const T& new_value);
OutputIterator replace_copy
    (InputIterator first, InputIterator last,
     OutputIterator result,
     const T& old_value, const T& new_value);
OutputIterator replace_copy_if
    (InputIterator first, InputIterator last,
     OutputIterator result,
     Predicate pred, const T& new_value);
```

We have discussed the *replace* algorithm in Section 1.10. Recall that, with a given *int* array *a* defined as

```
int a[5] = {8, 8, 8, 0, 8};
```

we can replace all values 8 with the value 1 by executing

```
replace(a, a+5, 8, 1);
```

which gives array the contents 1, 1, 1, 0, 1.

There is also the function *replace_if*, which takes a different third argument: a unary predicate specifying a condition. All elements that meet this condition are replaced with the value given by the fourth argument. The following program demonstrates this *replace_if* algorithm:

```
// repl_if.cpp: Replace every non-zero element of an
//                  array with 1.

#include <iostream>
#include <algorithm>
using namespace std;

bool nonzero(int x) {return x != 0;}

int main()
{   int a[5] = {10, 20, 30, 0, 40};
    replace_if(a, a+5, nonzero, 1);
    cout << "After replace_if:\n";
    copy(a, a+5, ostream_iterator<int>(cout, " "));
    cout << endl;
    return 0;
}
```

All nonzero elements in {10, 20, 30, 0, 40} are set to 1, so that the program gives the following output:

```
After replace_if:
1 1 1 0 1
```

The two algorithms *replace_copy* and *replace_copy_if* are very similar to *replace* and *replace_if*. Instead of replacing elements of the original container, they first copy the given container to another one and then perform the replacements in that copy, leaving the original container unchanged. The third argument of these functions indicates the start of the container that will be the result of these copying and replacing operations, as the following program demonstrates:

```cpp
// replcopy.cpp: replace_copy and replace_copy_if.
#include <iostream>
#include <vector>
#include <algorithm>
using namespace std;

bool not_ten(int x) {return x != 10;}

int main()
{   int a[5] = {10, 20, 20, 10, 40};
    cout << "Array a:\n";
    copy(a, a+5, ostream_iterator<int>(cout, " "));
    vector<int> v;
    vector<int>::iterator i;
    replace_copy(a, a+5, inserter(v, v.begin()),
        20, 49);
    cout << "\n\nAfter the execution of\n   replace_copy"
        "(a, a+5, inserter(v, v.begin()), 20, 49);"
        "\nvector v has the following contents:\n";
    copy(v.begin(), v.end(),
        ostream_iterator<int>(cout, " "));
    replace_copy_if(a, a+5, v.begin(), not_ten, 99);
    cout << "\n\nAfter the execution of\n"
        "   replace_if_copy(a, a+5, v.begin(), "
        "not_ten, 99);"
        "\nvector v has the following contents:\n";
    copy(v.begin(), v.end(),
        ostream_iterator<int>(cout, " ")); cout << endl;
    return 0;
}
```

In this program, the vector *v* is initially empty, so we use insert mode in the first call to *replace_copy*. This algorithm is used to copy array *a* to vector *v*, but replacing all values 20 with 49. Then the *replace_copy_if* algorithm does the same, except that it replaces all values unequal to 10 with 99 and works in overwrite mode. The output of this program shows this very clearly:

```
Array a:
10 20 20 10 40

After the execution of
    replace_copy(a, a+5, inserter(v, v.begin()), 20, 49);
vector v has the following contents:
10 49 49 10 40

After the execution of
    replace_if_copy(a, a+5, v.begin(), not_ten, 99);
vector v has the following contents:
10 99 99 10 99
```

7.2.6 Remove

```
ForwardIterator remove
   (ForwardIterator first, ForwardIterator last,
    const T& value);
ForwardIterator remove_if
   (ForwardIterator first, ForwardIterator last,
    Predicate pred);
OutputIterator remove_copy
   (InputIterator first, InputIterator last,
    OutputIterator result, const T& value);
OutputIterator remove_copy_if
   (InputIterator first, InputIterator last,
    OutputIterator result, Predicate pred);
```

We have discussed the *remove* and *remove_if* algorithms in Section 1.13. As the names *remove_copy* and *remove_copy_if* of the other two versions indicate, these perform the remove operation in a copy rather than in the original container. Since this is similar to what we have seen with *replace_copy* and *replace_copy_if*, we will not discuss these two copying versions of *remove* in detail.

7.2.7 Fill

```
void fill
   (ForwardIterator first, ForwardIterator last,
    const T& value);
void fill_n
   (ForwardIterator first, Size n, const T& value);
```

The *fill* algorithm puts a given value in all elements of a given range. As usual, we specify this range for *fill* by supplying two iterators. The *fill_n* algorithm works in the same way as *fill*, but with this function we specify a range by means of one iterator and the number of elements to be filled. The following program uses both algorithms:

```cpp
// fill.cpp: The algorithms fill and fill_n.
#include <iostream>
#include <algorithm>
using namespace std;

int main()
{   int a[5];
    fill(a, a+5, 123);
    copy(a, a+5, ostream_iterator<int>(cout, " "));
    cout << endl;
    fill_n(a, 2, 456);
    copy(a, a+5, ostream_iterator<int>(cout, " "));
    cout << endl;
    return 0;
}
```

This program first assigns the value 123 to all five elements of array *a*. Then it replaces the first two elements with 456, as the output of this program shows:

```
123 123 123 123 123
456 456 123 123 123
```

This second version *fill_n* would be superfluous for arrays, vectors and deques, since these containers provide random access, so that we can replace

```
fill_n(i, n, x);
```

with

```
fill(i, i+n, x);
```

with these containers. However, such a replacement is not possible for lists: if *i* is an iterator for a list, the expression $i + n$ is invalid.

7.2.8 Generate

```
void generate
    (ForwardIterator first, ForwardIterator last,
     Generator gen);
void generate_n
    (ForwardIterator first, Size n,
     Generator gen);
```

Instead of using a fixed value to fill a container, we may want to generate a value for each element. We can do this by using the *generate* algorithm. The third argument of this algorithm is a function (or a function object). The following program places the values 10, 12, 14, 16 and 18 in the array *a*:

```
// generate.cpp: The generate algorithm.
#include <iostream>
#include <algorithm>
using namespace std;

struct funobj {
   int i;
   funobj(): i(8){}
   int operator()(){return i += 2;}
};

int main()
{  int a[5];
   generate(a, a+5, funobj());
   copy(a, a+5, ostream_iterator<int>(cout, " "));
   cout << endl;   // Output: 10 12 14 16 18
   return 0;
}
```

Note the use of a function object that contains not only an operator( ) function but also an *int* member *i* and a constructor. This member variable *i* is equal to 8 when the function object is created, and it is increased by 2 each time the operator() function is called, so that this function successively returns the values 10, 12, 14, 16 and 18. The program fills array *a* in the same way if we use the function

```
int fun()
{   static int i=8;
    return i += 2;
}
```

instead of class *funobj* and, at the same time, call *generate* in the following way:

```
generate(a, a+5, fun);
```

However, there is a subtle difference: if we used two such calls to *generate*, the variable *i* would not be reset to 8 for the second call in this modified program (with the third argument *fun*), while *i* would be reset to this value if we duplicated the call to *generate* with *funobj*( ) as its third argument.

If *a* is a vector or a deque (containing at least five elements), we can replace this call with

```
generate(a.begin(), a.begin()+5, fun);
```

However, we cannot do this for a *list*, since the plus operator is not defined for bidirectional iterators. Fortunately, there is an algorithm *generate_n*, which also works for a list. The following program shows two unrelated differences with the previous one: it is based on the function *fun* instead of the function object *funobj*(), and it uses the *generate_n* algorithm so that we can easily specify a range of five elements in a list:

```
// gen_n.cpp: The generate_n algorithm.
#include <iostream>
#include <algorithm>
#include <list>
using namespace std;

int fun()
{   static int i=8;
    return i += 2;
}

int main()
{   list<int> a(5);
    generate_n(a.begin(), 5, fun);
    copy(a.begin(), a.end(),
        ostream_iterator<int>(cout, " "));
    cout << endl;  // Output: 10 12 14 16 18
    return 0;
}
```

7.2.9 Unique

```
ForwardIterator unique
    (ForwardIterator first, ForwardIterator last);
ForwardIterator unique
    (ForwardIterator first, ForwardIterator last,
     BinaryPredicate binary_pred);
OutputIterator unique_copy
    (InputIterator first, InputIterator last,
     OutputIterator result);
OutputIterator unique_copy
    (InputIterator first, InputIterator last,
     OutputIterator result,
     BinaryPredicate binary_pred);
```

The *unique* algorithm eliminates all consecutive duplicate elements of a range. This algorithm is similar to *remove* in that it does not alter the size of the container. Obviously, this would not be possible with an array anyway, but the sizes of vectors, deques and lists will not become smaller either. Incidentally, if we want to use this algorithm for lists, we had better use the list member function *unique* instead for reasons of efficiency. Recall that we have discussed this list member function in Section 3.5.

The *unique* algorithm returns the new logical end, as the following program demonstrates:

```
// unique1.cpp: First unique algorithm.
#include <iostream>
#include <algorithm>
using namespace std;

int main()
{   int a[10] = {3, 4, 3, 3, 4, 4, 5, 3, 3, 3}, *p;
    p = unique(a, a+10);
    cout << "New logical contents of array a:\n";
    copy(a, p, ostream_iterator<int>(cout, " "));
    cout << endl;
    return 0;
}
```

This program produces the following output:

```
New logical contents of array a:
3 4 3 4 5 3
```

Instead of applying the equality operator == to successive elements, we may want to use some other binary predicate. To do this, we can use another algorithm with the same name, but with this predicate as its third argument. The following program uses this algorithm to remove each element that is one higher than its immediate predecessor:

```cpp
// unique2.cpp: Second unique algorithm.
//      Remove v[i+1] if it is equal to v[i] + 1.
#include <iostream>
#include <vector>
#include <algorithm>
using namespace std;

bool onehigher(int x, int y){return x + 1 == y;}

int main()
{   int a[10] = {3, 4, 3, 1, 6, 7, 7, 7, 8, 4};
    vector<int> v;
    vector<int>::iterator i;
    for (int k=0; k<10; k++) v.push_back(a[k]);
    i = unique(v.begin(), v.end(), onehigher);
    cout << "Logical contents of v:\n";
    copy(v.begin(), i, ostream_iterator<int>(cout, " "));
    cout << "\nv.size() = " << v.size() << endl;
    return 0;
}
```

Initially, the values

```
3 4 3 1 6 7 7 7 8 4
```

are placed in the vector v. Since $v[1]$ (= 4) is one higher than its predecessor $v[0]$, this first element 4 will not appear in the result. Neither will $v[5]$ (= 7), because its predecessor $v[4]$ is equal to 6. Although it seems at first that 8 will be removed because it follows 7, this is not the case: after removal of all values 7, the value 8 follows the value 6 and will therefore not disappear, as this output shows:

```
Logical contents of v:
3 3 1 6 8 4
v.size() = 10
```

Note that the size of vector is still 10, but only the subrange [$v.begin()$, i) forms the logical contents. This situation is similar to a character array, of which only the first portion, ending with '\0', is actually used.

If, after the call $i = unique(...)$, we want to reduce $v.size()$ = 10 to its new logical length $i - v.begin()$ = 6, we can use the *erase* member function as follows:

```cpp
v.erase(i, v.end());
```

There are also two functions *unique_copy*, which are similar to the two *unique* functions, except that they produce their result in a copy of the original container. We could have used one of these *unique_copy* versions very well in program *unique2.cpp*. Instead of

```
vector<int> v;
vector<int>::iterator i;
for (int k=0; k<10; k++) v.push_back(a[k]);
i = unique(v.begin(), v.end(), onehigher);
```

we could have used the simpler fragment

```
vector<int> v(10, 0);
vector<int>::iterator i;
i = unique_copy(a, a+10, v.begin(), onehigher);
```

After this modification, the program gives the same output as the original version.

The other *unique_copy* function is similar to our first version of *unique*. It simply tests if two consecutive elements are equal. We could use this version, for example, as follows:

```
i = unique_copy(a, a+10, v.begin());
```

7.2.10 Reverse

```
void reverse
    (BidirectionalIterator first,
     BidirectionalIterator last);
void reverse_copy
    (BidirectionalIterator first,
     BidirectionalIterator last, OutputIterator result);
```

Recall that we have discussed the *reverse* algorithm in Section 1.10. There is also the *reverse_copy* version, which does not modify the given range, but places its elements in reverse order in another container, as the following program shows:

```
// rcopy.cpp: The reverse_copy algorithm places
//            the result in a different container.

#include <iostream>
#include <algorithm>
using namespace std;

int main()
{   int a[3] = {10, 20, 30}, b[3];
    reverse_copy(a, a+3, b);
    copy(b, b+3, ostream_iterator<int>(cout, " "));
    cout << endl; // Output: 30 20 10
    return 0;
}
```

7.2.11 Random Shuffle

```
void random_shuffle
    (RandomAccessIterator first,
     RandomAccessIterator last);
void random_shuffle
    (RandomAccessIterator first,
     RandomAccessIterator last,
     RandomNumberGenerator& rand);
```

The *random_shuffle* algorithm places the elements of a given range in a random order, as the following program illustrates:

```
// rshuffle.cpp: Random shuffle.
#include <iostream>
#include <algorithm>
using namespace std;

int main()
{   int a[6] = {10, 20, 30, 40, 50, 60};
    random_shuffle(a, a+6);
    copy(a, a+6, ostream_iterator<int>(cout, " "));
    cout << endl;
    return 0;
}
```

When this program was executed, it produced the following output:

```
40 10 60 30 20 50
```

When executed repeatedly, the program is consistent in producing this output. This is because the *random_shuffle* algorithm is based on a pseudo random-number generator, which works in the same way (using the same 'seed value') each time we start the program.

There is also a version of *random_shuffle* that takes such a random-number generating function as its third argument. This enables us to obtain different output each time we run the program. The random-number generating function must take an *int* argument n and return an *int* value in the range $[0, n)$, randomly chosen. We can provide this function as a function object, as the following program shows:

```
// rshuff1.cpp: Random shuffle; generator of our own.
#include <iostream>
#include <stdlib.h>
#include <time.h>
#include <algorithm>
using namespace std;
```

```
struct myrandom {
   myrandom()
   {  srand((unsigned int)time(NULL));
   }
   int operator()(int n){return rand() % n;}
};

int main()
{  int a[6] = {10, 20, 30, 40, 50, 60};
   random_shuffle(a, a+6, myrandom());
   copy(a, a+6, ostream_iterator<int>(cout, " "));
   cout << endl;
   return 0;
}
```

When this program was executed for the first time, it produced the output

```
50 10 30 20 40 60
```

When executed for the second time, the output was different:

```
10 30 60 40 20 50
```

Incidentally, instead of using the *myrandom* class, we can define the function

```
int randfun(int n)
{  static int first = 1;
   if (first)
   {  srand((unsigned int)time(NULL));
      first = 0;
   }
   return rand() % n;
}
```

provided we also replace the call to *random_shuffle* with the following one:

```
random_shuffle(a, a+6, randfun);
```

7.2.12 Partition

```
void partition
   (BidirectionalIterator first,
    BidirectionalIterator last, Predicate pred);
void stable_partition
   (BidirectionalIterator first,
    BidirectionalIterator last, Predicate pred);
```

The *partition* algorithm splits a range into two partitions. It places all elements that satisfy a given condition before those that do not. In the following program, the array *a* contains integers, some of which are less than 50, while others are not. We then use *partition*, supplied with the predicate 'less than 50', to rearrange the elements of *a* in such a way that all elements less than 50 will precede those that are at least 50. The partition algorithm returns an iterator value, which refers to the first element of the second partition:

```
// partitio.cpp: The partition algorithm.
#include <iostream>
#include <algorithm>
using namespace std;

bool below50(int x){return x < 50;}

int main()
{   int a[8] = {70, 40, 80, 20, 50, 60, 50, 10};
    int *p = partition(a, a+8, below50);
    copy(a, p, ostream_iterator<int>(cout, " "));
    cout << "   ";
    copy(p, a+8, ostream_iterator<int>(cout, " "));
    cout << endl;
    return 0;
}
```

Array *a* contains three elements (40, 20 and 10) that are less than 50. After the call to *partition* these three elements appear at the beginning, as the following output shows:

```
10 40 20    80 50 60 50 70
```

The value $p - a$ is equal to the length (3) of the first partition. One of the two partitions can be empty. For example, we would have $p - a = 8$ if we replaced 50 with 1000 in the function *below*50, and $p - a = 0$ if we replaced 50 with 0.

Note that the elements 40, 20 and 10 that are less than 50 do not preserve their original relative order, and neither do the other elements (70, 80, 50, 60, 50). If we want this to happen, all we have to do is to use *stable_partition* instead of *partition*, writing

```
int *p = stable_partition(a, a+8, below50);
```

By doing this, we obtain the following output, in which the elements in each partition appear in the same order as they did in the original sequence:

```
40 20 10    70 80 50 60 50
```

The *stable_partition* algorithm will normally take more computing time than the *partition* algorithm; if this were not the case, the designers of STL would no doubt have introduced only a stable partitioning algorithm.

As you may know, partitioning a sequence is the basis for a well-known sorting method, known as *quicksort*.

7.3 Sorting-Related Algorithms

The algorithms of this section are related to sorting. There are two versions of them: one based on the less-than operator and the other on a compare function of our own.

7.3.1 Less-Than and Other Comparison Operations

Algorithms that are related to sorting depend on a relation operation, for which we frequently use the 'less than' operator <. Instead, we can use the 'greater than' operator >, or use some other binary comparison predicate. However, we must be very careful with the latter. The chosen predicate must be similar to < with regard to the following requirements:

1. If $x < y$ and $y < z$, then $x < z$.
2. If $x < y$, then $y < x$ is false.

Note that 1. and 2. also hold if we replace < with > but not if we replace it with <= ==, or !=.

7.3.2 Sort

```
void sort
    (RandomAccessIterator first,
     RandomAccessIterator last);
void sort(RandomAccessIterator first,
          RandomAccessIterator last, Compare comp);
```

We have discussed the *sort* algorithm based on the < operator in Section 1.4, and the other, a more general one using a specified compare predicate, in Sections 1.11 and 1.12. Recall that we can sort an *int* array *a* of *N* elements in ascending order by writing

```
sort(a, a+N);
```

while we write

```
sort(a, a+N, greater<int>());
```

to sort the array in descending order.

7.3.3 Stable Sort

```
void stable_sort
    (RandomAccessIterator first,
     RandomAccessIterator last);
void stable_sort
    (RandomAccessIterator first,
     RandomAccessIterator last, Compare comp);
```

To discuss the notion of stable sort, it is desirable to sort records rather than integers. The following program sorts an array of 20 records, each consisting of a string and an integer. The strings will be used as keys, so after sorting they will appear in lexicographical order. Before sorting, the values 10, 11, ..., 29 are stored in the *num* members of the array elements $a[0]$, $a[1]$, ..., $a[19]$. We do this by defining the less-than operator for records $a[i]$ and $a[j]$ in such a way that $a[i] < a[j]$ if the string $a[i].s$ lexicographically precedes $a[j].s$:

```
// sortrec.cpp: Sorting records.
#include <iostream>
#include <string>
#include <algorithm>
using namespace std;

struct rectype
{   string s; int num;
    bool operator<(const rectype &b)const
    {   return s < b.s;
    }
};

int main()
{   const int N = 20;
    string t[20] =
    {"Judy", "John", "John", "Judy", "John",
     "Judy", "Paul", "Judy", "Paul", "Mary",
     "Mary", "John", "Judy", "Paul", "John",
     "Paul", "Judy", "John", "Judy", "Judy"};
    int k;
    rectype a[N];
    for (k=0; k<N; k++)
    {   a[k].s = t[k]; a[k].num = 10 + k;
    }
    sort(a, a+N);
    for (k=0; k<N; k++)
    {   cout << a[k].s << " "
             << a[k].num << (k % 5 == 4 ? "\n" : "   ");
    }
    return 0;
}
```

This program produced the following output:

```
John 11   John 12   John 14   John 27   John 24
John 21   Judy 29   Judy 28   Judy 26   Judy 22
Judy 17   Judy 15   Judy 13   Judy 10   Mary 20
Mary 19   Paul 18   Paul 23   Paul 25   Paul 16
```

The names appear in lexicographical order in this sorted list. As you can already see on the first of the four output lines, the numbers associated with the same key *John* do not appear in ascending order. Since they were in ascending order before sorting took place, we see that their relative order is not preserved. For example, the records (*John*, 27) and (*John*, 24) appear in that order in the sorted array, while initially (*John*, 24) preceded (*John*, 27). This is because the *sort* algorithm is not *stable*. There is also a stable version, however. To use this, we simply replace the above call to *sort* with this one:

```
stable_sort(a, a+N);
```

After this program modification, we obtain the following output:

```
John 11   John 12   John 14   John 21   John 24
John 27   Judy 10   Judy 13   Judy 15   Judy 17
Judy 22   Judy 26   Judy 28   Judy 29   Mary 19
Mary 20   Paul 16   Paul 18   Paul 23   Paul 25
```

Records with equal 'keys' (such as those containing the name *John*) now appear in ascending order of the numbers; in other words, the relative order of such records is preserved.

As with the *sort* algorithm, there is a version of *stable_sort* that takes a predicate as its third argument.

7.3.4 Partial Sort

```
void partial_sort
    (RandomAccessIterator first,
     RandomAccessIterator middle,
     RandomAccessIterator last);
void partial_sort
    (RandomAccessIterator first,
     RandomAccessIterator middle,
     RandomAccessIterator last, Compare comp);
RandomAccessIterator partial_sort_copy
    (InputIterator first, InputIterator last,
     RandomAccessIterator result_first,
     RandomAccessIterator result_last);
RandomAccessIterator partial_sort_copy
    (InputIterator first, InputIterator last,
     RandomAccessIterator result_first,
     RandomAccessIterator result_last, Compare comp);
```

If we are interested only in the first *n* elements of the completely sorted sequence, where *n* is less than the sequence length, we need not sort the whole sequence. In the following program, elements $a[0]$, $a[1]$, $a[2]$ and $a[3]$ obtain the same values as they would if the entire array were sorted:

```
// partsort.cpp: Partial sorting.
#include <iostream>
#include <string>
#include <algorithm>
using namespace std;

int main()
{   int a[10] = {9, 8, 7, 6, 5, 4, 3, 2, 1, 0};
    partial_sort(a, a+4, a+10);
    for (int k=0; k<10; k++)
       cout << a[k] << (k == 3 ? "    " : " ");
    cout << endl;
    return 0;
}
```

This program produces the following output:

```
0 1 2 3    9 8 7 6 5 4
```

The elements after the first four can appear in any order: although in this example they are in the same order as they were initially, we must not count on this.

There is also a version of *partial_sort* that takes a predicate for comparisons as its fourth argument, which is similar to what we have seen with the *sort* algorithm.

If we want to place the results in a range different from the given one, we can use the two *partial_sort_copy* algorithms. Again, there is one that depends on the less-than operator and one that takes an additional argument, a predicate for comparisons. The first, based on <, is used in the following program:

```
// partsrt1.cpp: partial_sort_copy.
#include <iostream>
#include <algorithm>
using namespace std;

int main()
{   int a[10] = {9, 8, 7, 6, 5, 4, 3, 2, 1, 0},
        b[40], *p;
    p = partial_sort_copy(a, a+10, b, b+4);
    copy(b, p, ostream_iterator<int>(cout, " "));
    cout << endl;
    p = partial_sort_copy(a, a+10, b, b+40);
    copy(b, p, ostream_iterator<int>(cout, " "));
    cout << endl;
    return 0;
}
```

The algorithm *partial_sort_copy* is supplied with two ranges, one for 'input' and the other for 'output'. The smallest of these two ranges determines how many sorted elements will appear in the output range; in either case the function returns an iterator referring to the element just after the final one in the sorted (sub)range. The above program shows two situations. After the first call to *partial_sort_copy* we have $p - b = min(10, 4) = 4$, and after the second $p - b = min(10, 40) = 10$, as the following output illustrates:

```
0 1 2 3
0 1 2 3 4 5 6 7 8 9
```

7.3.5 *N*th Element

```
void nth_element
    (RandomAccessIterator first,
     RandomAccessIterator position,
     RandomAccessIterator last);
void nth_element
    (RandomAccessIterator first,
     RandomAccessIterator position,
     RandomAccessIterator last, Compare comp);
```

After a call to the *nth_element* algorithm with the iterator p as its second argument, the value of $*p$ is the same as it would be if the range in question were sorted. The following program illustrates this:

```
// nth_elt.cpp: The nth_element algorithm.
#include <iostream>
#include <algorithm>
using namespace std;

int main()
{   int a[10] = {4, 12, 9, 5, 6, 6, 6, 4, 8, 10};
    nth_element(a, a+2, a+10);
    copy(a, a+10, ostream_iterator<int>(cout, " "));
    cout << endl;
    return 0;
}
```

The output

```
4 4 5 6 6 6 9 12 8 10
```

of this program shows that the element $a[2]$ contains the value 5. The latter would also be the case if the array had been completely sorted, since then we would have obtained

```
4 4 5 6 6 6 8 9 10 12
```

Apart from the order, the new array contents are the same as the original one. Also, all elements before the 'pivot' $a[2] = 5$ are not greater than this pivot and all elements that follow are not less than it.

The three arguments of *nth_element* are random-access iterators. There is also a version that takes a fourth argument, which is a predicate for comparison. For example, if we replace the above call to *nth_element* with

```
nth_element(a, a+2, a+10, greater<int>());
```

we obtain the following output:

```
10 12 9 8 6 6 6 4 5 4
```

The point to be noticed is that $a[2] = 9$, which would also be the case if the array had been completely sorted in descending order. The elements that precede $a[2]$ are not less and those that follow are not greater than this element.

7.3.6 Binary Search

```
ForwardIterator lower_bound
   (ForwardIterator first, ForwardIterator last,
    const T& value);
ForwardIterator lower_bound
   (ForwardIterator first, ForwardIterator last,
    const T& value, Compare comp);
ForwardIterator upper_bound
   (ForwardIterator first, ForwardIterator last,
    const T& value);
ForwardIterator upper_bound
   (ForwardIterator first, ForwardIterator last,
    const T& value, Compare comp);
pair<ForwardIterator, ForwardIterator> equal_range
   (ForwardIterator first, ForwardIterator last,
    const T& value);
pair<ForwardIterator, ForwardIterator> equal_range
   (ForwardIterator first, ForwardIterator last,
    const T& value, Compare comp);
bool binary_search
   (ForwardIterator first, ForwardIterator last,
    const T& value);
bool binary_search
   (ForwardIterator first, ForwardIterator last,
    const T& value, Compare comp);
```

We will discuss four algorithms in this section: *lower_bound*, *upper_bound*, *equal_range* and *binary_search*. Our program will only demonstrate the versions that are based on the less-than operator <. For each of these four algorithms, there is also a version that takes an extra argument, which is a comparison predicate. All these algorithms assume the range in question to be sorted. The following program uses each of the four versions without this predicate argument:

```cpp
// bsearch.cpp: Binary search and related algorithms.

#include <iostream>
#include <algorithm>
using namespace std;

int main()
{   int a[10] = {3, 3, 5, 5, 5, 5, 5, 7, 8, 9}, *p, k;
    cout << "Array a:\n";
    for (k=0; k<10; k++) cout << k << " ";
    cout << endl;
    for (k=0; k<10; k++) cout << a[k] << " ";
    cout << endl;

    p = lower_bound(a, a+10, 5);
    cout << "p - a = " << p - a
         << " after p = lower_bound(a, a+10, 5);\n";

    p = lower_bound(a, a+10, 4);
    cout << "p - a = " << p - a
         << " after p = lower_bound(a, a+10, 4);\n";

    p = upper_bound(a, a+10, 5);
    cout << "p - a = " << p - a
         << " after p = upper_bound(a, a+10, 5);\n";

    pair<int*, int*> P(0, 0);
    P = equal_range(a, a+10, 5);
    cout <<
        "After P = equal_range(a, a+10, 5) we have:\n";
    cout << "  P.first  - a = " << P.first  - a << endl;
    cout << "  P.second - a = " << P.second - a << endl;

    bool b = binary_search(a, a+10, 5);
    cout << "Results of binary_search:\n";
    cout << "5 " << (b ? "" : "not ")
         << "found in array a.\n";
    b = binary_search(a, a+10, 4);
    cout << "4 " << (b ? "" : "not ")
         << "found in array a.\n";
    return 0;
}
```

This program produces the following output:

```
Array a:
0  1  2  3  4  5  6  7  8  9
3  3  5  5  5  5  5  7  8  9
p - a = 2 after p = lower_bound(a, a+10, 5);
p - a = 2 after p = lower_bound(a, a+10, 4);
p - a = 7 after p = upper_bound(a, a+10, 5);
After P = equal_range(a, a+10, 5) we have:
  P.first  - a = 2
  P.second - a = 7
Results of binary_search:
5 found in array a.
4 not found in array a.
```

As this output shows, *lower_bound* returns an iterator referring to the *first* position at which the given element can be inserted, so that the sequence remains sorted. For both values 5 and 4, this position is $a[2]$. Similarly, the call to *upper_bound* returns a value indicating that $a[7]$ is the *last* position at which the value 5 can reasonably be inserted.

The call to *equal_range* informs us that [2, 7) is the range of positions at which the value 5 can be inserted. If we had used the call

```
equal_range(a, a+10, 4);
```

both *P.first – a* and *P.second – a* would have been equal to 2, since $a[2]$ is the only position at which the value 4 can be inserted.

The algorithm *binary_search* merely informs us whether the given value has been found; it provides no information about where this value has been found or where it belongs if it is not found.

7.3.7 Merge

```
OutputIterator merge
   (InputIterator1 first1, InputIterator last1,
    InputIterator1 first2, InputIterator last2,
    OutputIterator result);
OutputIterator merge
   (InputIterator1 first1, InputIterator last1,
    InputIterator1 first2, InputIterator last2,
    OutputIterator result, Compare comp);
void inplace_merge
   (BidirectionalIterator first,
    BidirectionalIterator middle,
    BidirectionalIterator last);
void inplace_merge
   (BidirectionalIterator first,
    BidirectionalIterator middle,
    BidirectionalIterator last, Compare comp);
```

There are two versions of the *merge* algorithm, one of which we have discussed in Section 1.7. The other takes a sixth argument, which is a predicate. This version can be used to merge two ranges that are sorted in descending order, as the following program illustrates:

```
// merge1.cpp: Merging two ranges that are in
//                 descending order.
#include <iostream>
#include <algorithm>
#include <functional>
using namespace std;

int main()
{  int a[5] = {30, 28, 15, 13, 11},
       b[4] = {25, 24, 15, 12},
       c[9];
   merge(a, a+5, b, b+4, c, greater<int>());
   copy(c, c+9, ostream_iterator<int>(cout, " "));
   cout << endl;
   return 0;
}
```

This program produces the following output:

```
30 28 25 24 15 15 13 12 11
```

Recall that we would omit the last argument in the call to *merge* if the arrays *a* and *b* had been sorted in ascending order.

If the two given sorted sequences (in ascending order) are available in the same range [*first*, *last*), with one sorted sequence in [*first*, *middle*) and the other in [*middle*, *last*), we can use the following call to merge them in such a way that the result appears in the range [*first*, *last*):

```
inplace_merge(first, middle, last);
```

The following program demonstrates this algorithm *inplace_merge*:

```
// inplace.cpp: Merging two ranges in-place.
#include <iostream>
#include <algorithm>
using namespace std;

int main()
{  int a[7] = {2, 5, 8, /* Second range: */ 3, 4, 5, 9};
   inplace_merge(a, a+3, a+7);
   copy(a, a+7, ostream_iterator<int>(cout, " "));
   cout << endl;
   return 0;
}
```

This program produces the following output:

```
2 3 4 5 5 8 9
```

There is also a version of *inplace_merge* which takes a predicate as an extra argument, so we can supply our own comparison operator, as we did in program *merge*1.

7.3.8 Set Operations on Sorted Structures

```
bool includes
    (InputIterator1 first1, InputIterator1 last1,
     InputIterator2 first2, InputIterator2 last2);
bool includes
    (InputIterator1 first1, InputIterator1 last1,
     InputIterator2 first2, InputIterator2 last2,
     Compare comp);
OutputIterator set_union
    (InputIterator1 first1, InputIterator1 last1,
     InputIterator2 first2, InputIterator2 last2,
     OutputIterator result);
OutputIterator set_union
    (InputIterator1 first1, InputIterator1 last1,
     InputIterator2 first2, InputIterator2 last2,
     OutputIterator result, Compare comp);
OutputIterator set_intersection
    (InputIterator1 first1, InputIterator1 last1,
     InputIterator2 first2, InputIterator2 last2,
     OutputIterator result);
OutputIterator set_intersection
    (InputIterator1 first1, InputIterator1 last1,
     InputIterator2 first2, InputIterator2 last2,
     OutputIterator result, Compare comp);
OutputIterator set_difference
    (InputIterator1 first1, InputIterator1 last1,
     InputIterator2 first2, InputIterator2 last2,
     OutputIterator result);
OutputIterator set_difference
    (InputIterator1 first1, InputIterator1 last1,
     InputIterator2 first2, InputIterator2 last2,
     OutputIterator result, Compare comp);
OutputIterator set_symmetric_difference
    (InputIterator1 first1, InputIterator1 last1,
     InputIterator2 first2, InputIterator2 last2,
     OutputIterator result);
OutputIterator set_symmetric_difference
    (InputIterator1 first1, InputIterator1 last1,
     InputIterator2 first2, InputIterator2 last2,
     OutputIterator result, Compare comp);
```

We have used the algorithms *set_intersection* and *set_union* for set containers in Section 4.3. These algorithms are not restricted to set containers; they also apply to sorted sequence containers. The following algorithms are available for set operations on sorted structures: *include, set_union, set_intersection, set_difference* and *set_symmetric_difference*. For each of them there are two versions: one based on the less-than operator and the other on an additional argument, a compare predicate. The following program demonstrates these five algorithms, that is, their versions based on the less-than operator:

```
// setopstr.cpp: Set operations on sorted structures.
#include <iostream>
#include <algorithm>
using namespace std;

void show(const char *s, const int *begin,
          const int *end)
{   cout << s << " ";
    copy(begin, end, ostream_iterator<int>(cout, " "));
    cout << endl;
}

int main()
{   int a[4] = {1, 5, 7, 8}, b[3] = {2, 5, 8},
        sum[7], *pSumEnd,
        prod[4], *pProdEnd,
        dif[3], *pDifEnd,
        symdif[7], *pSymDifEnd;
    pSumEnd = set_union(a, a+4, b, b+3, sum);
    pProdEnd = set_intersection(a, a+4, b, b+3, prod);
    pDifEnd = set_difference(a, a+4, b, b+3, dif);
    pSymDifEnd = set_symmetric_difference(a, a+4, b, b+3,
        symdif);
    show("a:      ", a, a+4);
    show("b:      ", b, b+3);
    show("sum:    ", sum, pSumEnd);
    show("prod:   ", prod, pProdEnd);
    show("dif:    ", dif, pDifEnd);
    show("symdif:", symdif, pSymDifEnd);
    if (includes(a, a+4, b, b+3))
       cout << "a includes b.\n";
    else cout << "a does not include b.\n";
    if (includes(sum, pSumEnd, b, b+3))
       cout << "sum includes b.\n";
    else cout << "sum does not include b.\n";
    return 0;
}
```

This program produces the following output:

```
a:       1 5 7 8
b:       2 5 8
sum:     1 2 5 7 8
prod:    5 8
dif:     1 7
symdif: 1 2 7
a does not include b.
sum includes b.
```

The variable *sum* is used for the union of the sets *a* and *b*, the variable *prod* for their intersection. Any element occurring in *a* or *b* also occurs in *sum*; by contrast, *prod* consists of those elements that belong to both *a* and *b*. The difference *dif* of *a* and *b* consists of all elements that belong to *a* but not to *b*. Finally, the symmetric difference *symdif* consists of all elements that belong to exactly one of the sets *a* and *b* (not to both).

A set *S* is said to *include* a set *T* if all elements of *T* also belong to *S*. In our example, *a* does not include *b* because element 2 of *b* does not belong to *a*. A union of two sets includes each of these two sets, so that *sum* includes *b* in our example.

We can also use sequence containers, such as *a* and *b* in our example, to store 'multisets', and then apply the algorithms *set_union* etc. on them. The resulting 'union' is a set containing the maximum occurrences of every element, while the 'intersection' contains the minimum. For example, let us change the above program so that *a* is initialized slightly differently, replacing the second line of the *main* function with

```
{  int a[4] = {1, 1, 7, 8}, b[3] = {2, 5, 8},
```

After modifying the program modified in this way, we obtain the following output:

```
a:       1 1 7 8
b:       2 5 8
sum:     1 1 2 5 7 8
prod:    8
dif:     1 1 7
symdif: 1 1 2 5 7
a does not include b.
sum includes b.
```

7.3.9 Heap Operations

```
void push_heap
   (RandomAccessIterator first,
    RandomAccessIterator last);
void push_heap
   (RandomAccessIterator first,
    RandomAccessIterator last, Compare comp);
```

```
void pop_heap
   (RandomAccessIterator first,
    RandomAccessIterator last);
void pop_heap
   (RandomAccessIterator first,
    RandomAccessIterator last, Compare comp);
void make_heap
   (RandomAccessIterator first,
    RandomAccessIterator last);
void make_heap
   (RandomAccessIterator first,
    RandomAccessIterator last, Compare comp);
void sort_heap
   (RandomAccessIterator first,
    RandomAccessIterator last);
void sort_heap
   (RandomAccessIterator first,
    RandomAccessIterator last, Compare comp);
```

A *heap* is a particular organization of elements in a range [*start*, *end*), where *start* and *end* are random access operators. Let us begin with the following example of a heap:

```
i ->      0  1  2  3  4  5  6  7  8  9
a[i]  -> 80 70 60 40 50 45 30 25 20 10
```

In this example, and in any heap of ten elements, we have

$a[0]$ is not less than $a[1]$ and $a[2]$
$a[1]$ is not less than $a[3]$ and $a[4]$
$a[2]$ is not less than $a[5]$ and $a[6]$
$a[3]$ is not less than $a[7]$ and $a[8]$
$a[4]$ is not less than $a[9]$

In general, a container a with elements $a[0]$, $a[1]$, ..., $a[n-1]$ is said to satisfy the heap condition if

$a[i] \geq a[2 * i + 1]$
$a[i] \geq a[2 * i + 2]$

as far as these elements belong to the container. It follows that the first element ($a[0]$) of a heap is the largest. Heaps are useful as priority queues, discussed in Section 5.3, since there are operations to extract the first element and to insert a new element while maintaining the heap condition. Extracting the first element of an STL heap is done in two steps: we copy the first element in the usual way and then call the *pop_heap* algorithm. For example, using an array a, we can write

```
x = *a; pop_heap(a, a+10);
```

or, in the case of a vector or deque *v*:

```
x = *v.begin(); pop_heap(v.begin(), v.end());
```

The function *pop_heap* logically removes the first element of the container and then restores the heap condition.

Similarly, we insert a new element in these two steps: we add a new element at the end of the heap and then call the *push_heap* algorithm. For example:

```
a[9] = x; push_heap(a, a+10);
```

or

```
v.push_back(x); push_heap(v.begin(), v.end());
```

The *push_heap* algorithm restores the heap condition correctly if only the final element of a heap violates the heap condition. There is a more powerful (but more time-consuming) function, *make_heap*, which turns a sequential container (allowing for random access) into a heap. Finally, we can apply the *sort_heap* algorithm to a heap to obtain a sorted sequence, Note that this algorithm places the elements in ascending order, so they no longer satisfy the heap condition. The four heap algorithms just mentioned are used in the following program:

```cpp
// heapdemo.cpp: Demonstration of heap operations.
#include <iostream>
#include <algorithm>
using namespace std;

void show(const char *s, const int *begin,
          const int *end)
{   cout << s << endl << "   ";
    copy(begin, end, ostream_iterator<int>(cout, " "));
    cout << endl;
}

int main()
{   cout << "   ";
    for (int i=0; i<10; i++) cout << "  " << i;
    cout << endl;
    int a[10] = {20, 50, 40, 60, 80, 10, 30, 70, 25, 45};
    show("Initial contents of a:", a, a+10);
    random_shuffle(a, a+10);
    show("After random_shuffle(a, a+10):", a, a+10);
    make_heap(a, a+10);
    show("After make_heap(a, a+10):", a, a+10);
```

```
        int x = *a;
        pop_heap(a, a+10);
        show("After x = *a and pop_heap(a, a+10):", a, a+9);
        a[9] = x;
        push_heap(a, a+10);
        show("After a[9] = x and push_heap(a, a+10):",
            a, a+10);
        sort_heap(a, a+10);
        show("After sort_heap(a, a+10):", a, a+10);
        return 0;
    }
```

This program produces the following output, which illustrates our above discussion:

```
     0  1  2  3  4  5  6  7  8  9
Initial contents of a:
    20 50 40 60 80 10 30 70 25 45
After random_shuffle(a, a+10):
    30 25 45 40 50 80 60 70 20 10
After make_heap(a, a+10):
    80 70 60 40 50 45 30 25 20 10
After x = *a and pop_heap(a, a+10):
    70 50 60 40 10 45 30 25 20
After a[9] = x and push_heap(a, a+10):
    80 70 60 40 50 45 30 25 20 10
After sort_heap(a, a+10):
    10 20 25 30 40 45 50 60 70 80
```

After the call to *make_heap*, the first element is the largest, but the sequence is not completely in descending order; for example, 40 precedes 50. It is a heap, however, so that, after copying its first element (80) to the variable x, we can apply the *pop_heap* algorithm, to obtain a heap of only nine elements. This value 80 is then again inserted by first placing it at the end and then applying the *push_heap* algorithm to restore the heap condition. Finally, the heap is sorted by the special *sort_heap* algorithm, which benefits from the special arrangements of the elements and will therefore be faster than the general *sort* algorithm.

7.3.10 Minimum and Maximum

```
const T& min
    (const T& a, const T& b);
const T& min
    (const T& a, const T& b, Compare comp);
const T& max
    (const T& a, const T& b);
const T& max
    (const T& a, const T& b, Compare comp);
```

```
ForwardIterator min_element
   (ForwardIterator first, ForwardIterator last);
ForwardIterator min_element
   (ForwardIterator first, ForwardIterator last,
    Compare comp);
ForwardIterator max_element
   (ForwardIterator first, ForwardIterator last);
ForwardIterator max_element
   (ForwardIterator first, ForwardIterator last,
    Compare comp);
```

If we want to find the maximum or minimum of two objects for which the less-than operator < is defined, we can use the *min* and *max* algorithms, which may or may not be implemented in the following, well-known way:

```
#define min(x, y) ((x) < (y) ? (x) : (y))
#define max(x, y) ((x) < (y) ? (y) : (x))
```

There are also versions of *min* and *max* that take a third argument, used to specify our own comparison operation. The following program demonstrates *min* with two and *max* with three arguments:

```
// minmax.cpp: The min and max algorithms.

#include <iostream>
#include <algorithm>
using namespace std;

bool CompareLastDigit(int x, int y)
{  return x % 10 < y % 10;
}

int main()
{  int x = 123, y = 75, minimum, MaxLastDigit;
   minimum = min(x, y);
   MaxLastDigit = max(x, y, CompareLastDigit);
   cout << minimum << " " << MaxLastDigit << endl;
   return 0;    // Output: 75 75
}
```

In this program, the call to *min* returns 75, the smaller of the values 123 and 75. Then the call to *max* also returns 75 because the last digit (5) of this value is larger than that of 123.

To find the position of the minimum element of a sequence, we can use the algorithm *min_element*. The following program applies this algorithm both to an array and to a list:

```cpp
// min_elt.cpp: Minimum element of a sequence.

#include <iostream>
#include <list>
#include <algorithm>
using namespace std;

int main()
{   int a[5] = {10, 30, 5, 40, 20}, *p;
    list<int> L;
    L.insert(L.begin(), a, a+5);
    list<int>::iterator i;
    p = min_element(a, a+5);
    i = min_element(L.begin(), L.end());
    cout << *p << " " << *i << endl;    // Output: 5 5
    return 0;
}
```

There is also a version of *min_element* that takes a third argument, used to specify our own comparison operation, in the same way as we have just seen with the *min* and *max* algorithms. If we want to find the position of the maximum element of a sequence, we can use *max_element*, of which there are also two versions, similar to *min_element*.

7.3.11 Lexicographical Comparison

```cpp
bool lexicographical_compare
    (InputIterator1 first1, InputIterator1 last1,
     InputIterator2 first2, InputIterator2 last2);
bool lexicographical_compare
    (InputIterator1 first1, InputIterator1 last1,
     InputIterator2 first2, InputIterator2 last2,
     Compare comp);
```

We can compare sequences lexicographically, that is, in the way we compare text strings: their first elements determine the comparison result if these elements are different; otherwise, we compare their second elements if any, and so on. There are two *lexicographical_compare* algorithms: one with four parameters, based on the less-than operation <, and the other taking an additional argument for comparison, as the following program demonstrates:

```cpp
// lexcomp.cpp: Lexicographical comparison.
#include <iostream>
#include <algorithm>
#include <functional>
using namespace std;
```

```
int main()
{   int a[4] = {1, 3, 8, 2},
        b[4] = {1, 3, 9, 1};

    cout << "a: ";
    copy(a, a+4, ostream_iterator<int>(cout, " "));

    cout << "\nb: ";
    copy(b, b+4, ostream_iterator<int>(cout, " "));
    cout << endl;

    if (lexicographical_compare(a, a+4, b, b+4))
        cout << "Lexicographically, a precedes b.\n";

    if (lexicographical_compare(b, b+4, a, a+4,
        greater<int>()))
        cout <<
        "Using the greater-than relation, we find:\n"
        "b lexicographically precedes a.\n";
    return 0;
}
```

This program produces the following output:

```
a: 1 3 8 2
b: 1 3 9 1
Lexicographically, a precedes b.
Using the greater-than relation, we find:
b lexicographically precedes a.
```

If the sequences are of unequal length, an absent element in one sequence acts as one that 'precedes' any present element in the same position of the other container; for example, {1, 2} lexicographically precedes {1, 2, –5}, regardless of the comparison operator.

7.3.12 Permutation Generators

```
bool next_permutation
    (BidirectionalIterator first,
     BidirectionalIterator last);
bool next_permutation
    (BidirectionalIterator first,
     BidirectionalIterator last, Compare comp);
bool prev_permutation
    (BidirectionalIterator first,
     BidirectionalIterator last);
bool prev_permutation
    (BidirectionalIterator first,
     BidirectionalIterator last, Compare comp);
```

As its name indicates, the *next_permutation* algorithm generates the next permutation of a sequence. Successive calls to this algorithm make these permutations appear in lexicographical order, if possible. The *bool* return value indicates whether there is still another new permutation. The output of the following program will make this clear; it also shows how the *prev_permutation* algorithm generates the previous permutation:

```cpp
// permgen.cpp: Permutation generator, generating all
//               permutations of the sequence 1 2 3.

#include <iostream>
#include <algorithm>
using namespace std;

int main()
{   int a[3] = {1, 2, 3}, k;
    cout << "Six successive calls to next_permutation.\n"
        "Situation before call and value returned by "
        "call:\n";

    for (k=0; k<6; k++)
    {   copy(a, a+3, ostream_iterator<int>(cout, " "));
        bool b = next_permutation(a, a+3);
        cout << (b ? " true" : " false") << endl;
    };

    cout <<
        "Three successive calls to prev_permutation.\n"
        "Situation before call and value returned by "
        "call:\n";
    for (k=0; k<3; k++)
    {   copy(a, a+3, ostream_iterator<int>(cout, " "));
        bool b = prev_permutation(a, a+3);
        cout << (b ? " true" : " false") << endl;
    };
    return 0;
}
```

Starting with {1, 2, 3}, this program displays the contents of array *a* just *before* it calls the function *next_permuation*. There are six such calls. The first returns *true* and gives array *a* the contents {1, 3, 2}; the second also returns *true* and generates {2, 1, 3}, and so on. As you can see in the output below, the permutations appear in lexicographical order. When *a* = {3, 2, 1}, the sixth call to *next_permutation* returns *false* and gives *a* the original contents {1, 2, 3}. As for *prev_permutation*, this function works in the opposite way. It returns *false* when it changes {1, 2, 3} into {3, 2, 1} and *true* after transitions from {3, 2, 1} to {3, 1, 2}, from {3, 2, 1} to {2, 1, 3} and so on:

```
Six successive calls to next_permutation.
Situation before call and value returned by call:
1 2 3   true
1 3 2   true
2 1 3   true
2 3 1   true
3 1 2   true
3 2 1   false
Three successive calls to prev_permutation.
Situation before call and value returned by call:
1 2 3   false
3 2 1   true
3 1 2   true
```

There are also versions of *next_permutation* and *prev_permutation* that take an additional argument to specify a comparison operator.

7.4 Generalized Numeric Algorithms

To use algorithms discussed in this section we have to write

```
#include <numeric>
```

with the Draft C++ Standard. With HP STL we have to replace this line with the following one:

```
#include <algo.h>
```

7.4.1 Accumulate

```
T accumulate
   (InputIterator first, InputIterator last, T init);
T accumulate
   (InputIterator first, InputIterator last, T init,
    BinaryOperation binary_op);
```

We have discussed the *accumulate* algorithm in Section 2.1, using the programs *accum1.cpp*, *accum2.cpp* and *accum3.cpp*. Recall that we can use it not only to form the sum of a sequence, demonstrated in the program *accum1.cpp*, but also to 'accumulate' the values of its elements in other ways, as we have seen in the programs *accum2.cpp* and *accum3.cpp*. It should also be remembered that the accumulated value is added to the value given as the third argument.

7.4.2 Inner Product

```
T inner_product
    (InputIterator1 first1, InputIterator1 last1,
     InputIterator2 first2, T init);
T inner_product
    (InputIterator1 first1, InputIterator1 last1,
     InputIterator2 first2, T init,
     BinaryOperation1 binary_op1,
     BinaryOperation2 binary_op2);
```

The value

$$a_0 b_0 + a_1 b_1 + ... + a_{n-1} b_{n-1}$$

is said to be the *inner product* (or *dot product*) of the sequences $\{a_0, a_1, ..., a_{n-1}\}$ and $\{b_0, b_1, ..., b_{n-1}\}$. The simpler version of the two *inner_product* algorithm adds the inner product computed in this way to the value of the fourth argument, as the following program shows:

```
// inprod1.cpp: Simple inner product.

#include <iostream>
#include <numeric>
using namespace std;

int main()
{   int a[3] = {2, 20, 4},
        b[3] = {5, 2, 10}, inprod = 100;
    inprod = inner_product(a, a+3, b, inprod);
    cout << inprod << endl;
    // 100 + 2 * 5 + 20 * 2 + 4 * 10 = 190
    return 0;
}
```

As the comment near the end of this program shows, two arithmetic operators, + and *, are used. There is another version of *inner_product*, in which we supply a fifth and a sixth argument to specify our own operations, to be used instead of + and *, respectively. In the following program these are used to compute a product of powers:

```
// inprod2.cpp: Product of powers computed by inner
//                    product.

#include <iostream>
#include <numeric>
#include <functional>
using namespace std;
```

```
double power(int x, int n)
{   double y = 1;
    for (int k=0; k<n; k++) y *= x;
    return y;   // x raised to the power n
}

int main()
{   int a[3] = {2, 3, 5}, b[3] = {4, 1, 2}, product=1;
    product = inner_product(a, a+3, b, product,
        multiplies<double>(), power);
    cout << product << endl;
    // 1 * power(2, 4) * power(3, 1) * power(5, 2) =
    // 1 * 16 * 3 * 25 = 1200
    return 0;
}
```

7.4.4 Partial Sum

```
OutputIterator partial_sum
    (InputIterator first, InputIterator last,
     OutputIterator result);
OutputIterator partial_sum
    (InputIterator first, InputIterator last,
     OutputIterator result, BinaryOperation binary_op);
```

The *partial_sum* algorithm actually computes cumulative sums. For example, using the sequence {2, 3, 4, 8}, we can obtain the sequence {2, 5, 9, 17} by copying the first value, 2, and computing the other three elements as follows:

$$2 + 3 = \quad 5$$
$$5 + 4 = \quad 9$$
$$9 + 8 = \quad 17$$

The following program uses this *partial_sum* algorithm to compute the results we have just been discussing:

```
// partsum.cpp: Partial sum.
#include <iostream>
#include <numeric>
#include <algorithm>
using namespace std;

int main()
{   int a[4] = {2, 3, 4, 8}, b[4], *iEnd;
    iEnd = partial_sum(a, a+4, b);
    copy(b, iEnd, ostream_iterator<int>(cout, " "));
    cout << endl; // Output 2 5 9 17
    return 0;
}
```

The value returned by *partial_sum* is an iterator referring to the past-the-end element of the result; in other words, *iEnd* is equal to $b + 4$ in this program. The resulting sums may be placed in the original elements, so that we need not use two separate arrays *a* and *b*, but we can write

```
iEnd = partial_sum(a, a+4, a);
```

if the result is desired in array *a*.

There is a second version of *partial_sum*, which takes an additional argument to replace + with a different operation. For example, we can write

```
iEnd = partial_sum(a, a+4, b, multiplies<int>());
```

instead of the call to *partial_sum* in the program to obtain the output 2 6 24 192, since we have

$$2 \times 3 = 6$$
$$6 \times 4 = 24$$
$$24 \times 8 = 192$$

7.4.5 Adjacent Difference

```
OutputIterator adjacent_difference
    (InputIterator first, InputIterator last,
     OutputIterator result);
OutputIterator adjacent_difference
    (InputIterator first, InputIterator last,
     OutputIterator result,
     BinaryOperation binary_op);
```

The *adjacent_difference* algorithm computes the differences

$$d_i = a_i - a_{i-1}$$

where $i > 0$ and $d_0 = a_0$. For example, using $a = \{2, 3, 4, 8\}$, we obtain the differences $d = \{2, 1, 1, 4\}$, since $3 - 2 = 1$, $4 - 3 = 1$ and $8 - 4 = 4$. The algorithm returns the 'past the end' iterator value, as the following program shows:

```
// adjdif.cpp: Adjacent differences.

#include <iostream>
#include <numeric>
#include <algorithm>
using namespace std;
```

```
int main()
{  int a[4] = {2, 3, 4, 8}, d[4], *iEnd;
   iEnd = adjacent_difference(a, a+4, d);
   copy(d, iEnd, ostream_iterator<int>(cout, " "));
   cout << endl; // Output 2 1 1 4
   return 0;
}
```

It is possible to obtain the result in the given sequence; in that case we can write

```
iEnd = adjacent_difference(a, a+4, a);
```

There is also a version of *adjacent_difference* that takes an additional argument, so that we can specify an operation different from subtraction. For example, after the execution of

```
int a[4] = {2, 30, 150, 700}, b[4], *iEnd;
iEnd = adjacent_difference(a, a+4, b, divides<int>());
```

we have $b = \{2, 15, 5, 4\}$, since $30/2 = 15$, $150/30 = 5$ and $700/150 = 4$.

7.5 An Application: The Least Squares Method

We will now use the *accumulate* and *inner_product* algorithms for a well-known, practical problem. Suppose we are given a set of n number pairs (x_i, y_i), representing points in the xy-place, and we want to find a straight line, which reasonably fits through this set of points, as shown in Figure 7.1.

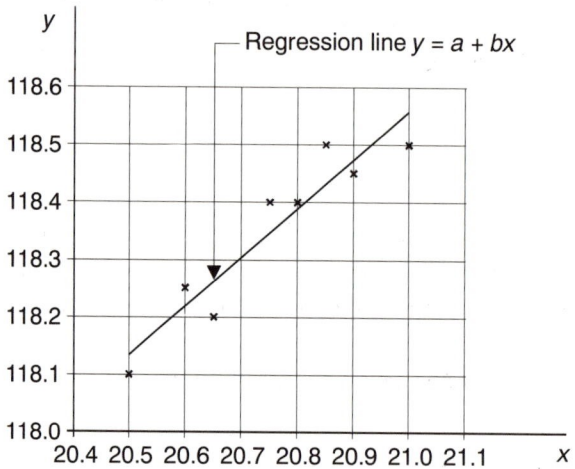

Figure 7.1 *Eight points and computed regression line*

The number of points (n) is arbitrary but must not be less than 2. The position of the points must not be such that the resulting line would be vertical; in particular, not all points must have the same x-value.

The n points will be given in an input file, the name of which will be entered by the user. For example, the eight points shown as crosses in Figure 7.1 are given in the following file *data.txt*:

```
20.5   118.1
20.6   118.25
20.65  118.2
20.75  118.4
20.8   118.4
20.85  118.5
20.9   118.45
21.0   118.5
```

The desired line, called a *regression line*, will be

$$y = a + bx$$

and the coefficients a and b are to be computed in such a way that the sum

$$\Sigma \, (y_i - y(i))^2 \quad (\text{where } y(i) = a + bx_i)$$

of the squares of the deviations has the smallest possible value. This *method of least squares* is due to Gauss, and the unknown coefficients a and b can be found by solving the following system of linear equations:

$$
\begin{aligned}
an &+ b\,\Sigma x_i &= \Sigma y_i \\
a\,\Sigma x_i &+ b\,\Sigma x_i^2 &= \Sigma x_i\, y_i
\end{aligned}
$$

Programming this with STL is attractive because:

- the *accumulate* algorithm makes it easy to compute Σx_i and Σy_i,
- the *inner_product* algorithm makes it easy to compute Σx_i^2 and $\Sigma x_i\, y_i$,
- sequence containers make it easy to store a variable number of x and y values.

As for the last point, it is not really necessary to store all these numbers, and this was not normally done in the early days of computing, when computer memory was very limited. We will assume that there is enough memory to store these numbers; this will enable us to display not only the desired coefficients a and b but also a list of differences

$$y_i - y(i)$$

where, as we have seen above, $y(i) = a + bx_i$. If we did not store all x and y values, we would have to scan the input file twice. Using type *vector<double>* both for x and y, we obtain the following program:

```cpp
// leastsq.cpp: Least-square method.
#include <iostream>
#include <fstream>
#include <iomanip>
#include <vector>
#include <numeric>
#include <string>
using namespace std;
typedef vector<double> array;

int ReadPoints(ifstream &file, array &x, array &y)
{   double x1, y1;
    while (file >> x1 >> y1)
    {   x.push_back(x1); y.push_back(y1);
    }
    return x.size();
}

int ComputeCoeff(const array &x, const array &y,
        double &a, double &b)
{   double sx=0, sx2=0, sy=0, sxy=0;
    sx = accumulate(x.begin(), x.end(), sx);
    sy = accumulate(y.begin(), y.end(), sy);
    sx2 = inner_product(x.begin(), x.end(),
        x.begin(), sx2);
    sxy = inner_product(x.begin(), x.end(),
        y.begin(), sxy);
    int n = x.size();
    double D = n * sx2 - sx * sx;
    if (D != 0)
    {   a = (sy * sx2 - sx * sxy)/D;
        b = (n * sxy - sx * sy)/D;
        return 1;
    }   else return 0;
}

void ShowComputedPoints(const array &x, const array &y,
        double a, double b)
{   cout << "\n          x        yGiven  yComputed\n\n"
        << setiosflags(ios::fixed);
    int n = x.size();
    for (int i=0; i<n; i++)
        cout << setw(10) << setprecision(2)<< x[i]
            << " " << setw(10) << y[i]
            << " " << setw(10) << a + b * x[i] << endl;
}
```

```
int main()
{   array x, y;
    double a, b;
    string FileName;
    cout << "Input file: ";
    cin >> FileName;
    ifstream file(FileName.c_str());
    if (!file)
    {   cout << "Cannot open input file.\n";
        return 1;
    }
    int n = ReadPoints(file, x, y);
    cout << "n = " << n << endl;
    if (n < 2)
    {   cout << "Too few points.\n";
        return 1;
    }
    if (ComputeCoeff(x, y, a, b) == 0)
    {   cout << "Vertical line not allowed.\n";
        return 1;
    }
    cout << "Regression line is y = a + bx, where\n"
        << "a = " << a << " and b = " << b << endl;
    ShowComputedPoints(x, y, a, b);
    return 0;
}
```

Using the above input file *data.txt*, we obtain the results shown below. The first two columns list the given points (*x*, *yGiven*), while the first and the third columns represent the points (*x*, *yComputed*), lying on the regression line in Figure 7.1:

```
Input file: data.txt
n = 8
Regression line is y = a + bx, where
a = 100.8 and b = 0.845528
```

x	yGiven	yComputed
20.50	118.10	118.13
20.60	118.25	118.22
20.65	118.20	118.26
20.75	118.40	118.34
20.80	118.40	118.39
20.85	118.50	118.43
20.90	118.45	118.47
21.00	118.50	118.56

Type of initial values

You may wonder why initial values such as the third argument in

```
sx = accumulate(x.begin(), x.end(), sx);
```

are specified in this book as (initialized) variables, since we might as well have written

```
sx = accumulate(x.begin(), x.end(), 0.0);
```

in which case it would not have been necessary to give *sx* the initial value 0 in its definition. This last call of *accumulate* is correct because 0.0 is of the type *double*. Curiously enough, the program gives wrong results if, in this call, we replace 0.0 with 0, of type *int*. A simple way of avoiding any such problems with constants of a wrong type is writing the same variable as we use to store the result. This principle applies to both *accumulate* and *inner_product*.

8

An Application: Very Large Numbers

8.1 Introduction

This chapter will be very different from the previous ones. We will discuss a useful class, *large*, based on STL and providing arithmetic operations on very large numbers. Besides a rather complex implementation file, *large.cpp*, there will be a corresponding header *large.h*, and two application programs. Program *large-dem.cpp* will demonstrate the available operations. After this, we will discuss a more interesting application, *largepi.cpp*, which computes the mathematical constant π to an arbitrary number of digits.

This subject is also discussed in a previous book, *Algorithms and Data Structures in C++* (see Bibliography), but without using STL. Our current solution will be more elegant and simpler, thanks to the STL vector container. As discussed in Section 3.7, this makes it possible to omit a copy constructor and an assignment operator. The *new* and *delete* operators will not occur in this chapter (while *new* occurs as many as eight times in the original version of *large.cpp* and once in the original version of *largepi.cpp*).

Number representation

Our integers of arbitrary length, will be stored as binary numbers. It will be convenient to view these numbers as written in the number system with radix $B = 2^n$, where n is the word length. We will therefore group contiguous sequences of n

bits together. This is similar to the usual practice of grouping sequences of four bits together to write bit sequences as hexadecimal numbers. The number of bits used for a *large* number will always be a multiple of n. With the 32-bit *int* type (that is, $n = 32$ and *sizeof*(*int*) = 4), the 'digits' range from 0 to $2^{32} - 1 = 4\,294\,967\,295$.

If we increase the latter value by 1, we can no longer store the result in one 'digit', so we need two 'digits', using 64 bits. We implement each number as a vector of *unsigned int* elements, together with a *bool* value *neg*, with is *true* if the number in question is negative and *false* if it is positive or zero. Each vector element will contain one 'digit', ranging from 0 to 2^{n-1}. With 32-bit integers, the vector size used to store a value x will therefore be:

$$0 \quad \text{if } x = 0$$
$$1 \quad \text{if } \; 0 \; < |x| < 2^{32}$$
$$2 \quad \text{if } 2^{32} \leq |x| < 2^{64}$$
$$3 \quad \text{if } 2^{64} \leq |x| < 2^{96}$$
$$4 \quad \text{if } 2^{96} \leq |x| < 2^{128}$$

and so on. The class *large* will provide the many operations, most of which are also available for standard arithmetical types:

- Arithmetic operations +, −, *, /, % (and a function *divide* to combine / and %).

- Binary shift operations << and >>.

- Each of these seven operators combined with assignment, giving +=, −=, *=, /=, %=, <<=, >>=.

- The usual overloaded output and input operators << and >>.

- Assignment =.

- Comparison ==, !=, <, >, <=, >=.

- The unary negation operator −.

- The functions *abs* for the absolute value, *sqrt* for the square root and *power* for exponentiation.

- Conversion to *large* from each of the types *int*, *unsigned int*, *long* and from the conventional C character string type *char** (provided such strings contain only decimal digits, possibly preceded by a minus sign).

- The function *num2char* to convert a *large* number to character representation, written, in reverse order, in a *vector<char>* object (see the note about portability at the end of this section).

Most of these operations are used in the demonstration program *largedem.cpp*, listed below.

```cpp
// largedem.cpp: Type large in action.
//      To be linked with large.cpp.
#include "large.h"

int main()
{  large a = -10000, b = 10000U, c = 2000000L,
       d = "100000000000000000000", // 20 zeros
       x, y, z, u;
   x = (a * b * b + 1) * c;
   x -= c;          // x = a * b * b * c
   x /= a * b;      // x = b * c
   y = large("1234567890123") % large("1234567890000");
   if (x == b * c && y == large(123))
      cout << "Arithmetic OK" << endl;

   z = power(d, 100);   // d raised to the power 100
                        // = 10 raised to the power 2000
   u = sqrt(z);         // 10 raised to the power 1000
   if (u == power(large(10), 1000))
      cout << "u = '10 raised to the power 1000'"
           << endl;

   if (u < power(large(11), 1000) &&
       u > power(large(9), 1000))
      cout << "Comparisons OK" << endl;

   vector<char> s;
   u.num2char(s);
   cout << "First character in output of u: "
        << *(s.end() - 1) << endl;
   cout << "u consists of " << s.size()
        << " decimal digits." << endl;

   z = d << 100; // z = d * (2 to the power 100)
   if (z == d * power(large(2), 100) && (z >> 100) == d)
      cout << "Shift operations OK" << endl;
   cout << -d << endl;

   cout << "Enter a large number x: ";
   cin >> x;
   cout << "2 * x = " << 2 * x << endl;
   a = "123456789123456789"; b = "999888777666";
   large q, r;
   a.divide(b, q, r, true);
   if (q != a/b || r != a%b)
      cout << "Function 'divide' incorrect." << endl;
   return 0;
}
```

Here is a demonstration of this program:

```
Arithmetic OK
u = '10 raised to the power 1000'
Comparisons OK
First character in output of u: 1
u consists of 1001 decimal digits.
Shift operations OK
-100000000000000000000
Enter a large number x: 999888777666555444333222111
2 * x = 1999777555333110888666444222
```

This program shows that the class *large* makes computing with very large numbers easy. For example, the integer $d = 10^{20}$ is used to compute

$$z = d^{100} = 10^{2000}$$
$$u = \sqrt{z} = 10^{1000}$$

Then the message *Comparisons OK* is displayed after verifying these three conditions:

$$u = 10^{1000}$$
$$u < 11^{1000}$$
$$u > 9^{1000}$$

As for shift operations, the large number $d = 10^{20}$ is shifted 100 binary positions to the left, giving

$$z = 10^{20} \times 2^{100}$$

This is verified both by using the *power* function to compute 2^{100} and by shifting z back 100 positions to the right to see if this gives d again.

Portability

The programs in this chapter have been successfully tested with the following three STL versions, mentioned in Section 1.2:

(1)   Visual C++ (Version 5.0)
(2)   The SGI adaptation for Visual C++ 5.0 from Ouchida
(3)   Borland C++ (Version 5.2)

Since the *min* and *max* algorithms cause a problem with the above STL version (1), we use the following line to test whether this is being used:

```
#if (defined(_MSC_VER) && !defined(_SGI_MSVC))
```

8.2 The Implementation of Class *large*

The *#if* line we have just been discussing occurs in the following header *large.h*, which we have already used in the program *largedem.cpp*:

```
// large.h: Multi-precision integer arithmetic.
#include <iostream>
#include <vector>
#include <iterator>

using namespace std;

typedef unsigned int uint;
typedef vector<uint> vec;

class large {
public:
   large(const char *str);
   large(int i);
   large(uint i=0);
   large(long i);
   large operator-()const;
   large &operator+=(const large &y);
   large &operator-=(const large &y);
   large &operator*=(int y);
   large &operator*=(uint y);
   large &operator*=(large y);
   large &operator/=(const large &divisor);
   large &operator%=(const large &divisor);
   large &operator<<=(uint k);
   large &operator>>=(uint k);
   void divide(large denom,
      large &quot, large &rem, bool RemDesired)const;

   // Function num2char converts a large object x to
   // its character representation s, in reverse order:
   void num2char(vector<char> &s) const;
   int compare(const large &y)const;
private:
   vec P;
   bool neg;
   void SetLen(int n);
   void reduce();
   void DDproduct(uint A, uint B, uint &Hi,
      uint &Lo)const;
   uint DDquotient(uint A, uint B, uint d)const;
   void subtractmul(uint *a, uint *b, int n,
      uint &q)const;
```

```
      bool normalize(large &denom, large &num,
         int &x)const;
      void unnormalize(large &rem, int x,
         bool SecondDone)const;
};

large operator+(large x, const large &y);
large operator-(large x, const large &y);
large operator*(large x, const large &y);
large operator/(large x, const large &y);
large operator%(large x, const large &y);
large operator<<(large u, uint k);
large operator>>(large u, uint k);
ostream &operator<<(ostream &os, const large &x);
istream &operator>>(istream &os, large &x);

bool operator==(const large &x, const large &y);
bool operator<(const large &x, const large &y);
bool operator!=(const large &x, const large &y);
bool operator>(const large &x, const large &y);

large abs(large x);
large sqrt(const large &a);
large power(large x, uint n);

#if (defined(_MSC_VER) && !defined(_SGI_MSVC))
template <class T>
inline const T& min(const T& a, const T& b)
{  return a < b ? a : b;
}

template <class T>
inline const T& max(const T& a, const T& b)
{  return a < b ? b : a;
}
#endif
```

The meaning of most public members of this class should be clear from our discussion of the program *largedem.cpp*. Note that the only comparison operators we define are == and <. The four others (!=, >, <=, >=) are then defined by STL, as discussed in Section 2.8.

The only data members of this class are *P* and *neg*, defined just below the keyword *private* as

```
vec P;
bool neg;
```

As the typedef declarations at the top of the file show, type *vec* actually stands for *vector<unsigned int>*. Remember, *P* represents the absolute value of a *large* number, while *neg* indicates whether this is negative.

The original version of the class *large*, not based on STL, contained a pointer of type *uint** instead of *vec P*, and there were also two other data members, *len* and *Len*, indicating the logical and the physical length. They correspond to the STL member functions *size* and *capacity*, respectively (see Section 3.2). These two lengths are now completely taken care of by STL.

We will not discuss all programming details of the class *large*; there are some explanatory comments that may be helpful if you insist on knowing how everything works. After compilation, the following implementation file must be linked with programs that use the class *large*:

```
// large.cpp: Multi-precision integer arithmetic,
//      based on STL.
#include <iostream>
#include <strstream>
#include <iomanip>
#include <stdlib.h>
#include <limits.h>
#include <string>
#include <ctype.h>
#include "large.h"
const uint uintmax = UINT_MAX;
const int wLen = sizeof(uint) * 8;   // Number of bits
const int hLen = wLen/2;
const uint rMask = (1 << hLen) - 1;
const uint lMask = uintmax - rMask;
const uint lBit = uintmax - (uintmax >> 1);

// Either insert zeros or delete some elements
// at the end, that is, in high-order positions:
void large::SetLen(int LenNew)
{   int LenOld = P.size();
    if (LenNew > LenOld)
       P.insert(P.end(), LenNew - LenOld, 0); else
    if (LenNew < LenOld)
       P.erase(P.begin()+LenNew, P.end());
}

// Remove any leading zeros (at the end of vector P):
void large::reduce()
{   int L = P.size();
    while (L > 0 && P[L-1] == 0) L--;
    P.erase(P.begin() + L, P.end());
    if (L == 0) neg = 0;
}
```

```
// Some constructors:
large::large(const char *str)
{  bool Neg = *str == '-';
   int i = (Neg ? 1 : 0);
   *this = 0;
   while (str[i])
       *this = *this * 10 + (str[i++] - '0');
   neg = Neg;
   reduce();
}

large::large(int i)
{  if (i > 0) P.push_back(i); else
   if (i < 0) P.push_back(-i);
   neg = i < 0;
}

large::large(long L)
{  neg = L < 0;
   unsigned long UL = neg ? -L : L;
   if (UL != 0)
   {
#if LONG_MAX == INT_MAX
       // sizeof(long) == sizeof(int):
       P.push_back(uint(UL));
#else
       // sizeof(long) > sizeof(int):
       while (UL != 0)
       {  P.push_back(uint(UL & UINT_MAX));
          UL >>= wLen;
       }
#endif
   }
}

large::large(uint i)
{  neg = 0;
   if (i) P.push_back(i);
}

// Operator + defined in terms of +=, and so on:
large operator+(large x, const large &y){return x+=y;}
large operator-(large x, const large &y){return x-=y;}
large operator*(large x, const large &y){return x*=y;}
large operator/(large x, const large &y){return x/=y;}
large operator%(large x, const large &y){return x%=y;}
large operator<<(large u, uint k){return u <<= k;}
large operator>>(large u, uint k){return u >>= k;}
```

```
large large::operator-()const
{  large v = *this;
   if (v.P.size()) v.neg = !v.neg;
   return v;
}

large &large::operator+=(const large &y)
{  if (neg != y.neg) return *this -= -y;
   int i, Ly = y.P.size();
   uint d, carry = 0;
   // Result length = max. operand length + 1:
   SetLen(max(Ly, (int)P.size()) + 1);
   int L = P.size();
   for (i=0; i<L; i++)
   {  if (i >= Ly && carry == 0) break;
      d = P[i] + carry;
      // Reset 'carry' to zero unless last
      // addition caused another carry:
      carry = d < carry;
      if (i < Ly)
      {  P[i] = d + y.P[i];
         // Only if 'carry' is now zero (and d > 0)
         // can last addition cause a carry:
         if (P[i] < d) carry = 1;
      } else P[i] = d;
   }
   reduce();
   return *this;
}

large &large::operator-=(const large &y)
{  if (neg != y.neg) return *this += -y;
   if (!neg && y > *this || neg && y < *this)
      return *this = -(y - *this);
   int i, borrow = 0, Ly = y.P.size(), L = P.size();
   uint d;
   for (i=0; i<L; i++)
   {  if (i >= Ly && borrow == 0) break;
      d = P[i] - borrow;
      borrow = d > P[i];
      if (i < Ly)
      {  P[i] = d - y.P[i];
         if (P[i] > d) borrow = 1;
      } else P[i] = d;
   }
   reduce();
   return *this;
}
```

```
large &large::operator*=(int y)
{   bool Neg = y < 0;
    if (Neg) y = -y;
    *this *= uint(y);
    if (Neg)
        neg = !neg;
    return *this;
}

large &large::operator*=(uint y)
{   int len0 = P.size(), i;
    uint Hi, Lo, dig = P[0], nextdig = 0;
    SetLen(len0 + 1);
    for (i=0; i<len0; i++)
    {   // Compute double-digit product dig * y;
        // result is (Hi, Lo):
        DDproduct(dig, y, Hi, Lo);
        P[i] = Lo + nextdig;
        dig = P[i+1]; nextdig = Hi + (P[i] < Lo);
    }
    P[i] = nextdig;
    reduce();
    return *this;
}

large &large::operator*=(large y)
{   int L = P.size(), Ly = y.P.size();
    if (L == 0 || Ly == 0) return *this = 0;
    bool DifSigns = neg != y.neg;
    if (L + Ly == 2)
    // L = Ly = 1: single- or double-digit product:
    {   uint a = P[0], b = y.P[0];
        P[0] = a * b; // Try single-digit product
        if (P[0] / a != b)
        {   P.push_back(0);
            DDproduct(a, b, P[1], P[0]);
            reduce();
        }
        neg = DifSigns;
        return *this;
    }
    if (L == 1)  //  && Ly > 1
    {   uint digit = P[0];
        *this = y;          // Swap operands and
        *this *= digit;  // call operator*=(uint y)
    } else
    if (Ly == 1) //  && L > 1
    {   *this *= y.P[0]; // Call operator*=(uint y)
    } else
```

```
      // Both operand lengths L and Ly greater than 1:
      {  int lenProd = L + Ly, i, jA, jB;
         uint sumHi = 0, sumLo, Hi, Lo,
         sumLoOld, sumHiOld, carry=0;
         large x = *this;
         SetLen(lenProd); // Give *this length lenProd

         for (i=0; i<lenProd; i++)
         {  sumLo = sumHi; sumHi = carry; carry = 0;
            int max_jA = min(i, L-1);
            // jA <= i ensures jB >= 0
            // jA < L since only L digits in *this
            for (jA=max(0, i+1-Ly); jA<=max_jA; jA++)
            // jA > i - Ly ensures jB < Ly
            {  jB = i - jA;
               // Another digit product contributing to
               // position i (= jA + jB) of number product:
               DDproduct(x.P[jA], y.P[jB], Hi, Lo);
               sumLoOld = sumLo; sumHiOld = sumHi;
               sumLo += Lo;
               if (sumLo < sumLoOld)
                  sumHi++;
               sumHi += Hi; carry += (sumHi < sumHiOld);
            }
            P[i] = sumLo;
         }
      }
   reduce();
   neg = DifSigns;
   return *this;
}


large &large::operator/=(const large &divisor)
{  large r;
   // Divide *this by divisor, giving quotient in
   // *this; 0 indicates that remainder in r
   // need not be correct:
   divide(divisor, *this, r, 0);
   return *this;
}


large &large::operator%=(const large &divisor)
{  large q;
   // Divide *this by divisor, giving quotient in
   // q and remainder in *this; 1 indicates that
   // this remainder has to be correct:
   divide(divisor, q, *this, 1);
   return *this;
}
```

```
large &large::operator<<=(uint k)
{  int q = k / wLen; // Number of full words.
   if (q)
   {  int i;           // Increase length by q:
      SetLen(P.size() + q);

      // Shift *this by q words to the left:
      for (i=P.size()-1; i>=0; i--)
         P[i] = (i < q ? 0 : P[i - q]);
      k %= wLen;       // k is now the remaining
   }                   // number of shift positions.

   if (k)   // 0 < k < wLen:
   {  int k1 = wLen - k;
      uint mask = (1 << k) - 1;
      // mask: 00..011..1 (k one-bits)
      SetLen(P.size() + 1);

      // Each P[i] shifts k positions to the left
      // and is then ORed with k leftmost bits
      // of right neighbor P[i-1]:
      for (int i=P.size()-1; i>=0; i--)
      {  P[i] <<= k;
         if (i > 0)
            P[i] |= (P[i-1] >> k1) & mask;
      }
   }
   reduce();
   return *this;
}

large &large::operator>>=(uint k)   // Analogous
{  int q = k / wLen, L = P.size(); // to <<=
   if (q >= L){*this = 0; return *this;}
   if (q)
   {  for (int i=q; i<L; i++) P[i-q] = P[i];
      SetLen(L - q);
      k %= wLen;
      if (k == 0){reduce(); return *this;}
   }
   int n = P.size() - 1, k1 = wLen - k;
   uint mask = (1 << k) - 1;
   for (int i=0; i<=n; i++)
   {  P[i] >>= k;
      if (i < n) P[i] |= ((P[i+1] & mask) << k1);
   }
   reduce();
   return *this;
}
```

```
// compare returns: negative if *this < y,
// zero if *this == y, and positive if *this > y.
int large::compare(const large &y)const
{   if (neg != y.neg) return y.neg - neg;
    int code = 0, L = P.size(), Ly = y.P.size();
    if (L == 0 || Ly == 0) code = L - Ly; else
    if (L < Ly) code = -1; else
    if (L > Ly) code = +1; else
    for (int i = L - 1; i >= 0; i--)
    {   if (P[i] > y.P[i]) {code = 1; break;} else
        if (P[i] < y.P[i]) {code = -1; break;}
    }
    return neg ? -code : code;
}


// Double-digit product (Hi, Lo) = A * B:
void large::DDproduct(uint A, uint B,
                      uint &Hi, uint &Lo)const
{   uint hiA = A >> hLen, loA = A & rMask,
         hiB = B >> hLen, loB = B & rMask,
         mid1, mid2, old;
    Lo = loA * loB; Hi = hiA * hiB;
    mid1 = loA * hiB; mid2 = hiA * loB;
    old = Lo;
    Lo += mid1 << hLen;
    Hi += (Lo < old) + (mid1 >> hLen);
    old = Lo;
    Lo += mid2 << hLen;
    Hi += (Lo < old) + (mid2 >> hLen);
}

// Double-digit value (A, B) is divided by d:
uint large::DDquotient(uint A, uint B, uint d)const
{   uint left, middle, right, qHi, qLo, x, dLo1,
         dHi = d >> hLen, dLo = d & rMask;
    qHi = A/(dHi + 1);
    // This initial guess of qHi may be too small.
    middle = qHi * dLo;
    left = qHi * dHi;
    x = B - (middle << hLen);
    A -= (middle >> hLen) + left + (x > B); B = x;
    dLo1 = dLo << hLen;

    // Increase qHi if necessary:
    while (A > dHi || (A == dHi && B >= dLo1))
    {   x = B - dLo1;
        A -= dHi + (x > B);
        B = x;
        qHi++;
    }
```

```
      qLo = ((A << hLen) | (B >> hLen))/(dHi + 1);
      // This initial guess of qLo may be too small.
      right = qLo * dLo; middle = qLo * dHi;
      x = B - right;
      A -= (x > B);
      B = x;
      x = B - (middle << hLen);
      A -= (middle >> hLen) + (x > B);
      B = x;
      // Increase qLo if necessary:
      while (A || B >= d)
      {  x = B - d;
         A -= (x > B);
         B = x;
         qLo++;
      }
      return (qHi << hLen) + qLo;
}


// Subtract multiple q * b from a, where a and b
// are values of n digits. The remainder a - q * b
// will be less than b and must not be negative.
// The latter condition may require q to be
// decreased by 1:
void large::subtractmul(uint *a, uint *b, int n,
   uint &q)const
{  uint Hi, Lo, d, carry = 0;
   int i;
   for (i=0; i<n; i++)
   {  DDproduct(b[i], q, Hi, Lo);
      d = a[i];
      a[i] -= Lo;
      if (a[i] > d) carry++;
      d = a[i + 1];
      a[i + 1] -= Hi + carry;
      carry = a[i + 1] > d;
   }
   if (carry) // q was too large
   {  q--; carry = 0;
      for (i=0; i<n; i++)
      {  d = a[i] + carry;
         carry = d < carry;
         a[i] = d + b[i];
         if (a[i] < d)
            carry = 1;
      }
      a[n] = 0;
   }
}
```

```
// Normalize by shifting denom and num to the left,
// so that the leftmost position of denom is 1;
// both operands of num/denom shift by x bit positions:
bool large::normalize(large &denom, large &num,
    int &x)const
{   int r = denom.P.size() - 1;
    uint y = denom.P[r]; x = 0;
    while ((y & 1Bit) == 0){y <<= 1; x++;}
    denom <<= x; num <<= x;
    // Possibly second action according to C. J. Mifsud
    // (see Bibliography):
    if (r > 0 && denom.P[r] < denom.P[r-1])
    {   denom *= uintmax; num *= uintmax;
        return 1;
    }
    return 0;
}


// Undo the effect of normalizing (including Mifsud's
// correction if SecondDone == 1) to obtain the
// correct remainder:

void large::unnormalize(large &rem, int x, bool
    SecondDone)const
{   if (SecondDone) rem /= uintmax;
    if (x > 0) rem >>= x; else rem.reduce();
}


// Divide *this by denom, giving quot = num / denom,
// and, if RemDesired == 1, rem = num % denom:
void large::divide(large denom,
    large &quot, large &rem, bool RemDesired)const
{   int L = P.size(), Ld = denom.P.size();
    if (Ld == 0) {cout << "Zero divide.\n"; return;}
    bool QuotNeg = neg ^ denom.neg;
    int i, r, x = 0, n;
    bool RemNeg = neg, SecondDone = false;
    uint q, d;
    large num = *this;
    num.neg = denom.neg = 0;
    if (num < denom)
    {   quot = 0; rem = num; rem.neg = RemNeg; return;
    }
    if (Ld == 1 && L == 1)
    {   quot = uint(num.P[0]/denom.P[0]);
        rem = uint(num.P[0]%denom.P[0]);
        quot.neg = QuotNeg; rem.neg = RemNeg;
        return;
    }   else
```

```
        if (Ld == 1 && (denom.P[0] & lMask) == 0)
        {   // Denominator fits into a half word
            uint divisor = denom.P[0], dHi = 0,
                q1, r, q2, dividend;
            quot.SetLen(L);
            for (int i=L-1; i>=0; i--)
            {   dividend = (dHi << hLen) | (P[i] >> hLen);
                q1 = dividend/divisor; r = dividend % divisor;
                dividend = (r << hLen) | (P[i] & rMask);
                q2 = dividend/divisor;
                dHi = dividend % divisor;
                quot.P[i] = (q1 << hLen) | q2;
            }
            quot.reduce(); rem = dHi;
            quot.neg = QuotNeg; rem.neg = RemNeg;
            return;
        }
        large num0 = num, denom0 = denom;
        SecondDone = normalize(denom, num, x);
        r = denom.P.size() - 1; n = num.P.size() - 1;
        quot.SetLen(n - r);
        int Lq = quot.P.size();
        for (i=Lq-1; i>=0; i--) quot.P[i] = 0;
        rem = num;
        if (rem.P[n] >= denom.P[r])
        {   rem.SetLen(rem.P.size() + 1);
            n++;
            quot.SetLen(Lq + 1);
        }
        d = denom.P[r];
        for (int k=n; k>r; k--)
        {   q = DDquotient(rem.P[k], rem.P[k-1], d);
            subtractmul(&rem.P[k - r - 1], &denom.P[0],
                r + 1, q);
            quot.P[k - r - 1] = q;
        }
        quot.reduce(); quot.neg = QuotNeg;
        if (RemDesired)
        {   unnormalize(rem, x, SecondDone);
            rem.neg = RemNeg;
        }
    }

bool operator==(const large &x, const large &y)
{   return x.compare(y) == 0;
}
bool operator<(const large &x, const large &y)
{   return x.compare(y) < 0;
}
```

```
bool operator!=(const large& x, const large& y)
{  return x.compare(y) != 0;
}

bool operator>(const large& x, const large& y)
{  return x.compare(y) > 0;
}


// Function num2char converts a large object x to
// its character representation s, in reverse order.
void large::num2char(vector<char> &s) const
{  large x = *this;
   static uint p10 = 1, ip10 = 0;
   if (x.P.size() == 0) s.push_back('0'); else
   {  uint r;
      if (p10 == 1)
      {  while (p10 <= UINT_MAX/10)
         {  p10 *= 10;
            ip10++;
         }
      }  // p10 is the largest possible uint power of 10
         // LP10 = p10 = pow(10, ip10)
      large R, LP10 = p10;
      bool neg = x.neg;
      do
      {  x.divide(LP10, x, R, 1);
         r = (R.P.size() ? R.P[0] : 0);
         for (uint j=0; j<ip10; j++)
         {  s.push_back(char(r % 10 + '0'));
            r /= 10;
            if (r + x.P.size() == 0) break;
         }
      }  while (x.P.size());
      if (neg) s.push_back('-');
      // s contains string in reverse order
   }
}

ostream &operator<<(ostream &os, const large &x)
{  vector<char> s;
   x.num2char(s);
   vector<char>::reverse_iterator i;
   for (i=s.rbegin(); i != s.rend(); ++i) os << *i;
   return os;
}

istream &operator>>(istream &is, large &x)
{  char ch;
   x = 0;
```

```
    bool neg = 0;
    is >> ch;

    if (ch == '-')
    {   neg = 1;
        is.get(ch);
    }

    while (isdigit(ch))
    {   x = x * 10 + (ch - '0');
        is.get(ch);
    }

    if (neg) x = -x;
    is.putback(ch);
    return is;
}

large abs(large a)
{   if (a < 0)
        a = -a;
    return a;
}

large sqrt(const large &a)
{   large x = a, b = a, q;
    b <<= 1;

    while (b >>= 2, b > large(0))
        x >>= 1;

    while (x > (q = a/x) + 1 || x < q - 1)
    {   x += q;
        x >>= 1;
    }
    return x < q ? x : q;
}

large power(large x, uint n)
{   large y=1;
    while (n)
    {   if (n & 1)
            y *= x;
        x *= x;
        n >>= 1;
    }
    return y;
}
```

8.3 Computing the Mathematical Constant π

Although the class *large* is intended for large integers, we can also use it to approximate real numbers, provided we are prepared to do a little bookkeeping, also known as *scaling*. Let us demonstrate this by computing the mathematical constant π to an arbitrary number of decimals. A well-known way to do this is by using the formula

$$\pi = 16 \arctan \frac{1}{5} - 4 \arctan \frac{1}{139}$$

due to John Machin (1680–1752). Instead, we will use

$$\pi = 48 \arctan \frac{1}{18} + 32 \arctan \frac{1}{57} - 20 \arctan \frac{1}{239} \tag{1}$$

which will perform better because the smallest denominator (18) in it is greater than that (5) in Machin's formula. Advanced mathematicians who are interested in the calculation of π should consult *Pi and the AGM*, by Borwein and Borwein, for more sophisticated algorithms. Since we are focusing on programming, we will simply use the above equation based on three *arctan* values, without proving it. The same applies to the way we can approximate the *arctan* function by using only the algebraic operations +, −, *, / in the following series:

$$\arctan x = x - \frac{x^3}{3} + \frac{x^5}{5} - \frac{x^7}{7} + \dots \tag{2}$$

The user of our program will specify n, the desired number of decimal digits that follow the period. For example, π will be represented in the output as

```
3.
1415
```

if n is equal to 4. Since we are approximating real numbers by integers, we should be careful with the last one or two digits, avoiding errors related to the way we approximate the *arctan* function. We will therefore actually use the scale factor

$$TenPower = 10^{n+3} \tag{3}$$

and omit the final three digits when displaying the result. Instead of π, we will actually compute an integer, approximately equal to $TenPower \times \pi$.

According to (1), the variable x in (2) will only assume values $1/k$, for $k = 18$, 57 and 239. Multiplying (2) by a very large number N, we obtain the following approximation, where the second line contains only integer variables:

N arctan $x = N$ arctan $(1/k) \approx$

$$N/k - N/(3k^3) + N/(5k^5) - N/(7k^7) + \ldots = Atan(k, N) \qquad (4)$$

Here N is a very large integer and the division operator / denotes integer division (as it does in $39/5 = 7$). Because of this, the three dots in (4) denote only a finite number of terms $N/(ik^i)$, so that we can compute them all. It then follows from (1) that $TenPower \times \pi$ is approximately equal to the very large integer:

$Atan(18, 48 \times TenPower) +$

$Atan(57, 32 \times TenPower) -$

$Atan(239, 20 \times TenPower)$

The following program is based on this expression:

```
// largepi.cpp: Large integers used to compute pi.
//    To be linked with large.cpp.

#include <fstream>
#include <time.h>
#include <stdlib.h>
#include "large.h"

// For the computation of pi:
large Atan(uint k, const large &N)
{   // Computes N * atan(1.0/k) as a large integer
    large a = 0,
        w = N * k,
        zero = 0,
        k2 = k * k,
        i = -1,
        two = 2;
    cout << "k = " << k << endl;
    while (w != zero)
    {   a += (w /= k2)/(i += two);
        a -= (w /= k2)/(i += two);
    }
    return a;
}

void PiOutput(ostream &os, ofstream &ofile,
    const large &x, int n)
{   vector<char> s;
    x.num2char(s);
    // Characters of x in reverse order in s.
    vector<char>::reverse_iterator i;
    int k = 0;
    char ch;
```

```
      for (i=s.rbegin(); i != s.rend(); ++i)
      {   ch = *i;
          os << ch;
          if (ofile) ofile << ch;
          // k digits have been displayed after period.
          if (k == 0)
          {   os << "." << endl;
              if (ofile) ofile << "." << endl;
          } else
          if (k % 50 == 0)
          {   os << endl;
              if (ofile) ofile << endl;
          } else
          if (k % 10 == 0)
          {   os << " ";
              if (ofile) ofile << " ";
          }
          if (k++ == n) break;
      }
}

int main()
{   int n, m;
    cout << "Computation of pi. Number of decimals: ";
    cin >> n; m = n + 3;
    cout <<
        "Copy of output to file pi.txt desired (y/n)? ";
    char answer;
    cin >> answer;
    ofstream ofile;
    if (answer == 'Y' || answer == 'y')
        ofile.open("pi.txt");
    large TenPower, Pi;
    clock_t tStart, tEnd;
    tStart = clock();
    TenPower = power(5, m); TenPower <<= m;
        // Faster than TenPower = power(10, m);

    Pi = (Atan(18, TenPower * 48)
        + Atan(57, TenPower * 32)
        - Atan(239, TenPower * 20))/1000;

    tEnd = clock();
    cout << "Digits of pi:" << endl;
    PiOutput(cout, ofile, Pi, n);
    cout << "\nTime: " << (tEnd - tStart) << " ticks\n";
    return 0;
}
```

With n much larger than 1000, you will notice that the program takes some time. To show some progress, it is then desirable to display some intermediate output for each of the following steps:

1. Computing *TenPower* $= 10^m$, where $m = n + 3$;
2. Computing *Atan*(239, *TenPower* * 20);
3. Computing *Atan*(57, *TenPower* * 32);
4. Computing *Atan*(18, *TenPower* * 48);
5. Converting the *large* variable *Pi* to the n-digit character string for output.

In step 1, we benefit from the shift-left operation, realizing that 10^m is equal to $5^m \times 2^m$ so that we can compute 5^m and shift the result m binary positions to the left. Since the computing time required for multiplying *large* numbers depends on their length, we can compute 5^m faster than 10^m.

Steps 2, 3 and 4 are not necessarily taken in this order. If an expression of the form $f(\ ) - g(\ )$ is to be evaluated, the C++ language does not specify the order in which the calls to f and g take place. In this demonstration call g happens to precede call f.

After the user has entered the desired number of decimals, he or she can indicate whether or not a copy of the output is to be written to a textfile, *pi.txt*, Then, when starting each of the above steps 2, 3 and 4, the program shows this by displaying some text, as the output on the next page demonstrates.

This demonstration was done with a Pentium 166 computer, 32 MB RAM, and BC5, running in a DOS box under Windows 95. Since, with BC5, a tick is equivalent to 1 ms, this computation of π (excluding the output) to a thousand decimal digits is done in about 0.3 s. An experiment to compute 100 000 decimals of π with this program took about half an hour. The results were verified by comparing the final ten of these decimals (5493624646) with output obtained by Yasumasa Kanada from Tokyo, who, incidentally, computed as many as 10^9 decimals, using quite different software and hardware.

As mentioned in the beginning of this chapter, a previous book, *Algorithms and Data Structures in C++*, presents a class *large* similar to the one here, but not based on STL. Computing π with this previous version took about as much time as with the current one, based on STL. However, programming the class *large* without STL was much more costly in terms of programming time. Exaggerating, we may compare the difference between STL and non-STL programming by that between using high-level programming languages and assembly code. Although the latter can provide more efficient code, it is these days definitely unsuitable for most applications. Programmers who ignore STL for reasons of efficiency are similar to those in the 1960s who thought that serious programming could only be done in assembly code.

```
Computation of pi. Number of decimals: 1000
Copy of output to file pi.txt desired (y/n)? n
k = 239
k = 57
k = 18
Digits of pi:
3.
1415926535 8979323846 2643383279 5028841971 6939937510
5820974944 5923078164 0628620899 8628034825 3421170679
8214808651 3282306647 0938446095 5058223172 5359408128
4811174502 8410270193 8521105559 6446229489 5493038196
4428810975 6659334461 2847564823 3786783165 2712019091
4564856692 3460348610 4543266482 1339360726 0249141273
7245870066 0631558817 4881520920 9628292540 9171536436
7892590360 0113305305 4882046652 1384146951 9415116094
3305727036 5759591953 0921861173 8193261179 3105118548
0744623799 6274956735 1885752724 8912279381 8301194912
9833673362 4406566430 8602139494 6395224737 1907021798
6094370277 0539217176 2931767523 8467481846 7669405132
0005681271 4526356082 7785771342 7577896091 7363717872
1468440901 2249534301 4654958537 1050792279 6892589235
4201995611 2129021960 8640344181 5981362977 4771309960
5187072113 4999999837 2978049951 0597317328 1609631859
5024459455 3469083026 4252230825 3344685035 2619311881
7101000313 7838752886 5875332083 8142061717 7669147303
5982534904 2875546873 1159562863 8823537875 9375195778
1857780532 1712268066 1300192787 6611195909 2164201989

Time: 312 ticks
```

Bibliography

Ammeraal, L. (1995) *C++ for Programmers*, 2nd Edition, Chichester: John Wiley.

Ammeraal, L. (1996) *Algorithms and Data Structures in C++*, Chichester: John Wiley.

Borland International (1996) *Borland C++ Programmer's Guide*, Version 5, Scotts Valley, CA: Borland International, Inc.

Borwein, J. M., and P. B. Borwein (1987) *Pi and the AGM*, New York, NY:John Wiley.

Cormen, T. H., C. E. Leiserson, and R. L. Rivest (1991) *Introduction to Algorithms*, 5th Edition, Cambridge, MA: MIT Press.

Mifsud, C. J. (1970) *A multiple-precision division algorithm*, Comm. ACM, Vol. 13, Number 11 (November 1970), 666-668.

Musser, D. R., and A. Saini, (1995) *STL Tutorial and Reference Guide*, Reading, Mass.: Addison-Wesley.

Plauger, P. J. (1995) *The Standard Template Library*, Series of monthly articles on STL in: *C/C++ Users Journal*, December 1995 - , Boulder, CO: Miller Freeman.

Sedgewick, R. (1992) *Algorithms in C++*, Reading, MA: Addison-Wesley.

Stepanov, A., and M. Lee, (1994) *The Standard Template Library*, Palo Alto, CA: Hewlett-Packard Company.

Stroustrup, B. (1997) *The C++ Programming Language*, 3nd Edition, Reading, Mass.: Addison-Wesley.

Stroustrup, B. (1994) *The Design and Evolution of C++*, 2nd Edition, Reading, Mass.: Addison-Wesley.

Index